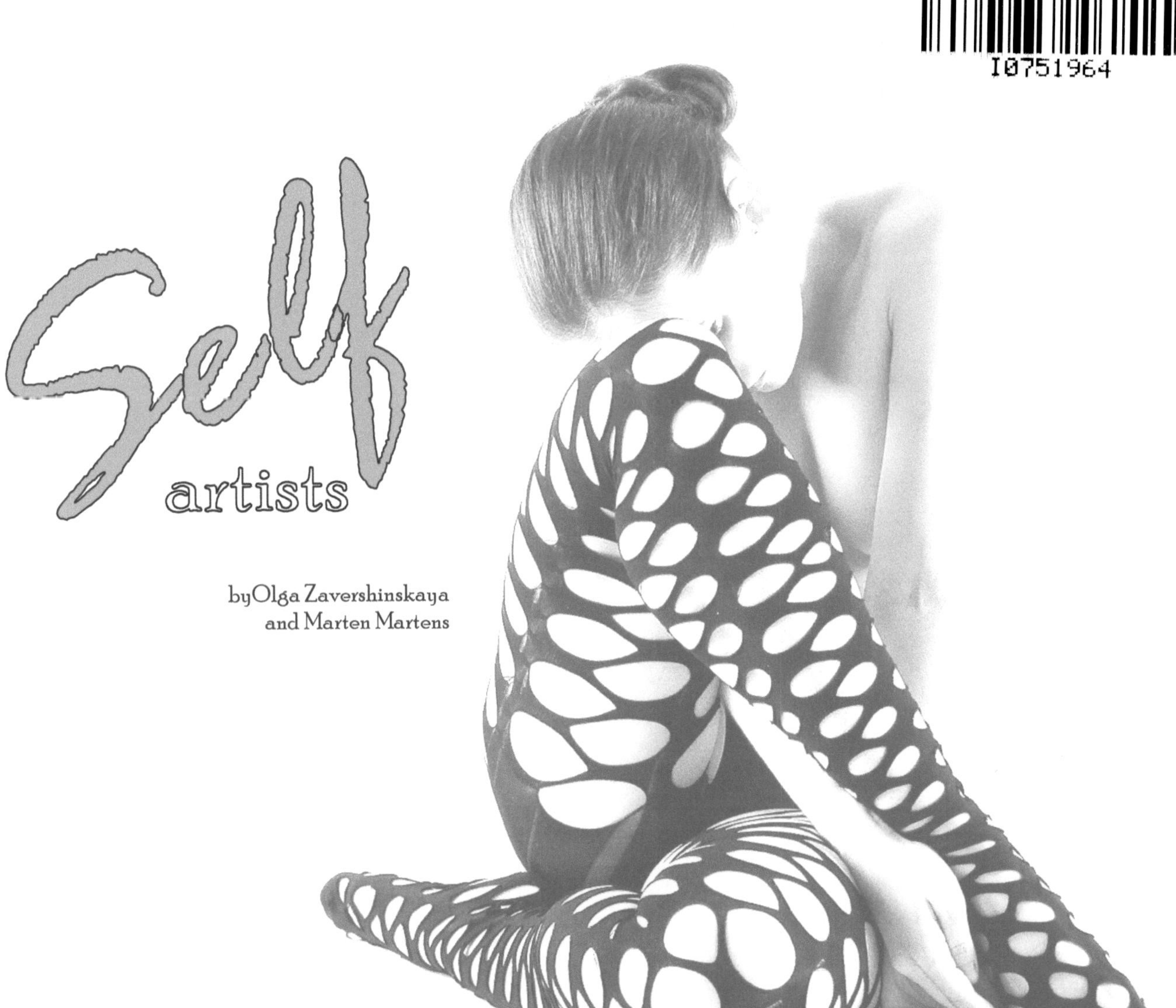
I0751964
Self
artists
byOlga Zavershinskaya
and Marten Martens

Published by Xin Publishing in May 2011
an imprint of Xin He Ltd.
Suite 404, 324 Regent Street
London, W1B 3HH
United Kingdom

Text Marten Martens
Design and layout Venjin He

ISBN: 978-0-9564897-7-7

Let each man exercise the art he knows.

.Aristophanes (450 BC - 388 BC)

Content

Revolution
of Art

Visionaries predicted that the Internet, in its inception, would spell a revolutionary shift in the way art is created and received. Those people were right, though not many would have predicted that the biggest impact would be on the way art is actually sold; with digital copies threatening artist's incomes and their rights to their own material, as the debate surrounding that issue appears to be a never ending saga.

A more positive shift and one that was predicted when the Internet was still in its infancy, is the democratization of art. The Internet allows everybody and anybody to be an artist; to create and publish their material within one minute without having to be, what would have been referred to before as, a 'member of the industry.' Unfortunately the sheer volume of amateur artists has saturated the web with their amateur music, poetry and painting, and so the consumer has become swamped and unable to find what is really of interest to them.

So is there art on the web?

Plenty! The difficult thing is finding the art which is both enjoyable and valuable. Galleries, publishing houses and music labels act in the real world like a quality filter that the online art community does not have, and although they are indeed marketing platforms, and they inevitably create a sort of mundane mainstream, they are integral in the art world beyond the web.

Then again the Internet generates its own sub-genres of art; spawned out of the World Wide Web itself and inextricably tied up in it; often untainted by any commercial interests: The new online-technologies open up exciting doors for everybody to be an artist, and at the same time introduce new platforms for communication.

Facebook, Twitter, Youtube and other social networks (but also dedicated communities like Flickr or Deviantart) are used to interact, to get in touch with others, to meet new and interesting people.

Of course this development has its flaws: Many social networks are rather dating sites, far too often these networks are merely a place of vanity or shameless self-manifestation. They also come with the risk of over-exposing yourself to a merciless public, of giving information that will never again vanish from the web and might influence even future job perspectives. Cases of cyber bullying and of course stalking are giving reason to be concerned and careful.

But, on the other hand, to a real artist bad publicity is better than no publicity and given the competitive nature of art on the web it is important to remain in the public's consciousness; hopefully through the art itself; its quality, mastery and perhaps, its genius.

The artist and art are often one and the same and by putting yourself on public view via MySpace or YouTube, artists are displaying their inner souls, and the Internet lends itself to criticism which the artist must accept and use, though it's difficult when your soul laid bare is the subject of at times negative feedback.

And similarly it works the other way. People's self-presentation on the web is becoming a type of art in itself, and just as the 1990's bloggers have moved into the realms of respected journalism, and singers like Sandi Thom who rose to stardom via YouTube are now celebrated artists, these pages represent new, hidden pearls of art, even if the message is as base as 'beauty.'

The Self Artist Project

This book contains extraordinary examples of art featuring the artists themselves found on the web. Individual thoughts and creative ideas really count on the web – and that is what this book is all about.
The artists featured are all young (because that is the Internet generation) and happy to put themselves on the line – online! – with their own ideas, lifestyles and their inner souls laid bare.

We hope you enjoy strolling through the art in this book which otherwise you might not have come across, tracing the paths of artists who walk a little out of step with the mainstream, but who create breath-taking art by revealing their inner most dreams and desires and expressing what is in their body and mind, and in their soul.

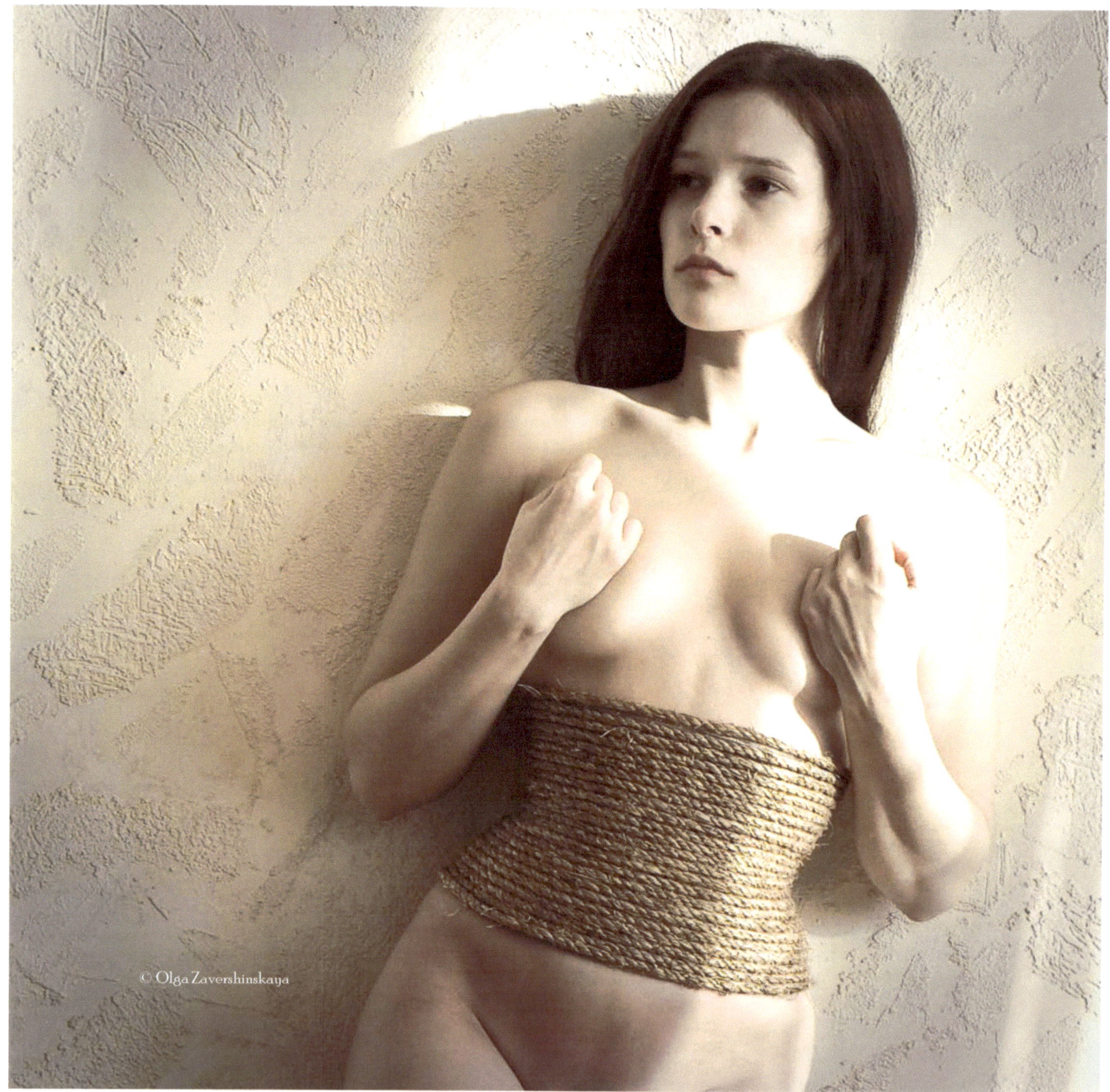
© Olga Zavershinskaya

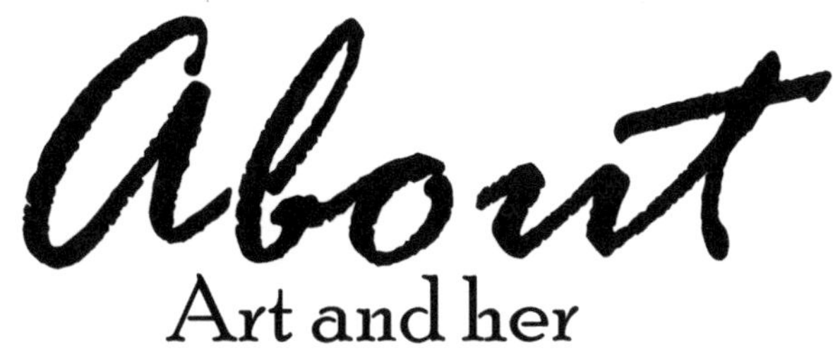

Art and her

Olga Zavershinskaya
Voronezh, Russia

Tools and methods

My field is digital photography. Equipments Nikkon D700, AF Nikkor 50mm/F 1.4, AF Nikkor 80-200mm/F 2.8, AF-S Nikkor 24-120mm/F 3.5-5.6. Studio stuff: tripod, remote control, timer, some studio flashes, reflectors, backgrounds. Post-processing used: Camera RAW 5.0, Photoshop CS4.

The relationship with own body

I use myself for different photo experiments just because my face and body are always at hand. Sometimes it is hard to find a model right in the moment you have an idea. Models can be busy, or don't like what you are going to do or they have bad days or thousand other reasons.

Behind the scenes

My "real life" is divided into three parts. Photography, photography and photography. Then comes my ownership of the 4th Dan in Taekwondo in which I am also a national referee. I'm also a post graduate student of the Department of forest transport and engineering geodesy.

Idea of self-expression

To create is absolutely natural for human beings. I do it just because I do it and not because I need to.

What led you to the world of Internet?

It is useful to meet a good friend or somebody who can be helpful or somebody to collaborate with. However, there is a chance to meet complete moron with mood disorder as well.

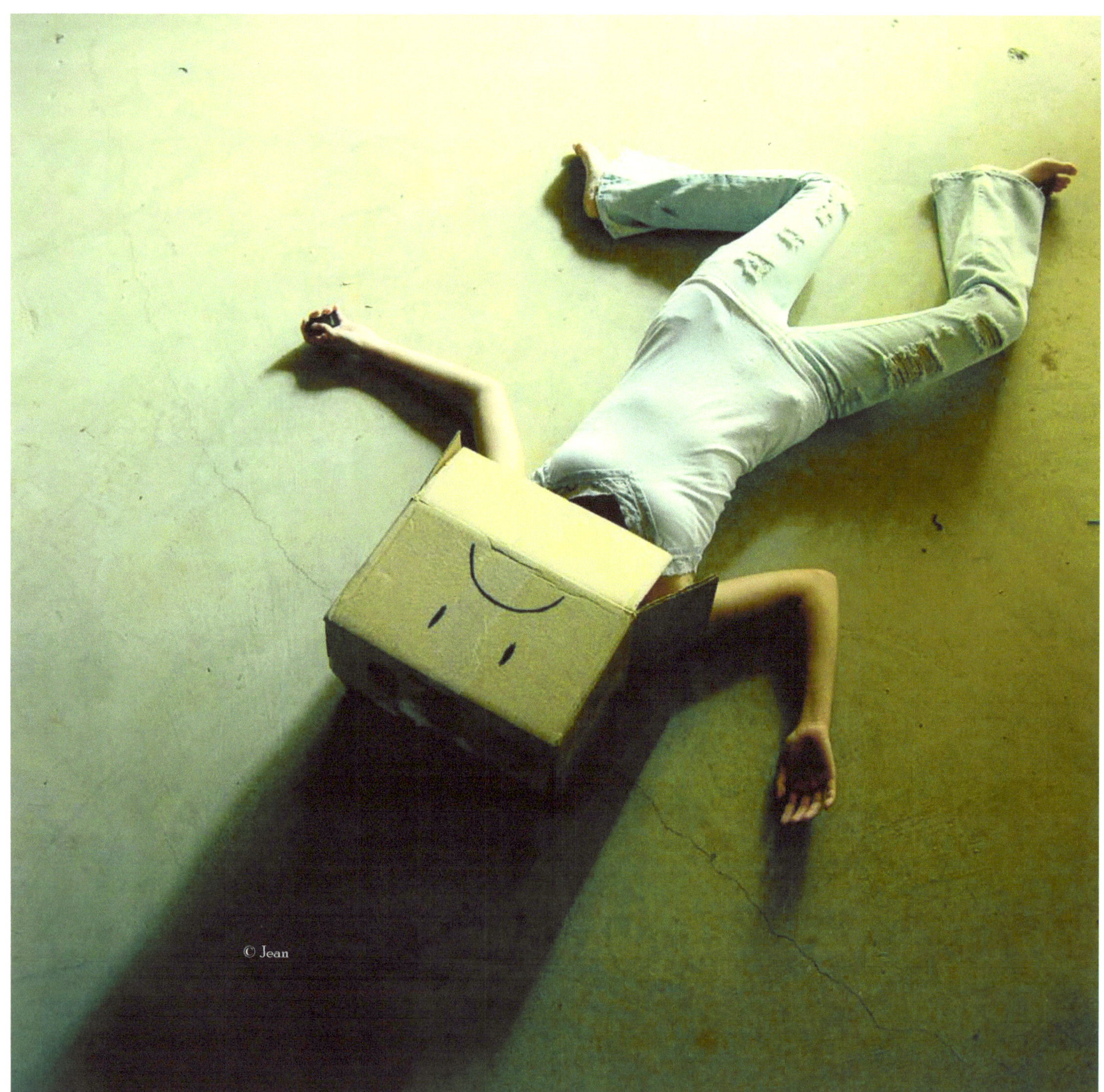
© Jean

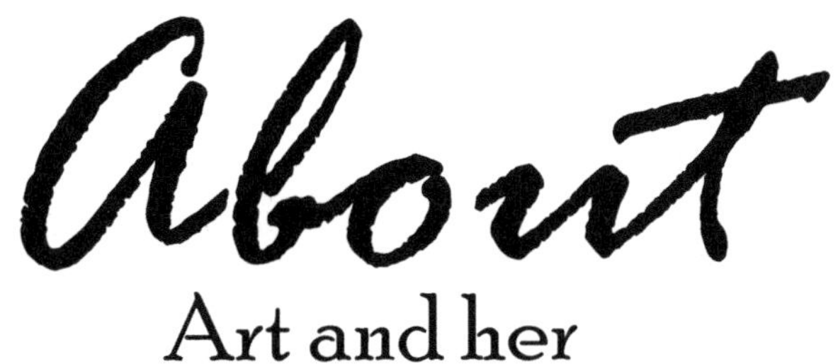

About

Art and her

Jean

Maryland, United States

Tools and methods

Currently, I work with the Nikon D80. As for the methods used in my work, I suppose they can be summarized as the following: I see it in my head and then I go recreate it. The recreation part varies depending on the piece but will always require a lot of patience and systematic repetition .

The relationship with own body

My body provides the means of actualizing my thoughts.

Behind the scenes

I am currently studying biomedical engineering and applied mathematics at Johns Hopkins University. I also intern at the Institute for Computational Medicine.

Idea of self-expression

Every man is an island that is incapable of directly communicating his thoughts and emotions. He will therefore attempt to communicate through self-expression in the hopes that others may be able to sympathize or even empathize. But no other will ever truly be able to comprehend these thoughts and emotions the way he does. I am no eloquent speaker. So I won't try to express myself through words. Instead I use my art as my attempt at a bridge off this island.

What led you to the world of Internet?

A friend once told me, "art isn't art until it's shared." Therefore, I use the internet to share my art. Over time, I've also come to use the internet to share photographic knowledge and philosophies.

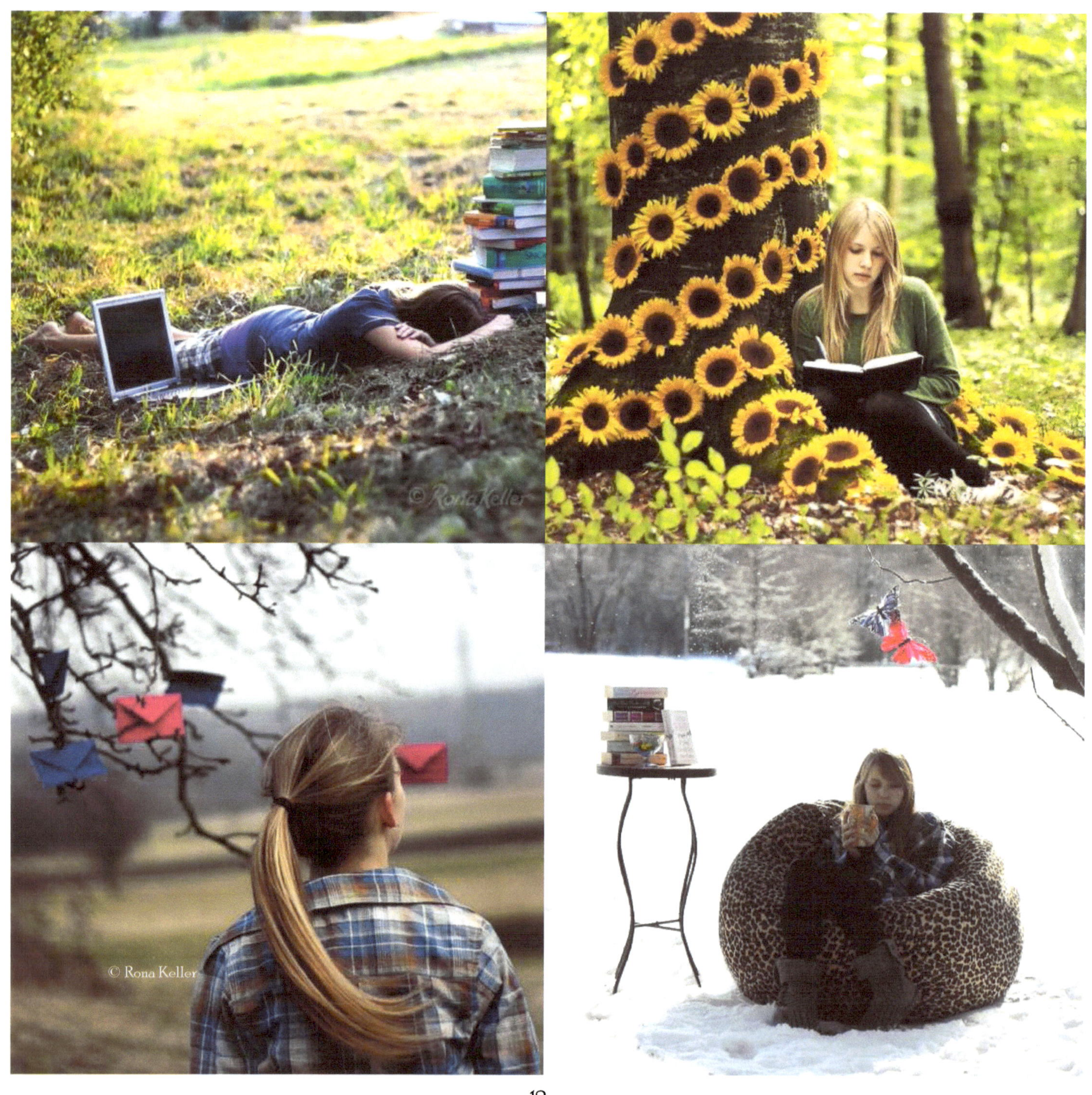
© Rona Keller
© Rona Keller

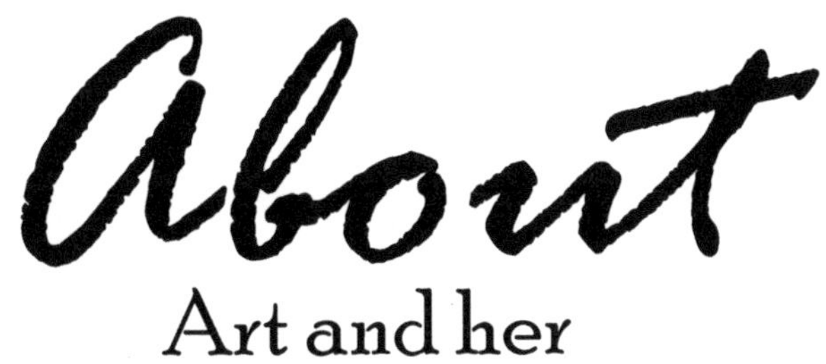

Art and her

Rona Keller

Gomaringen, Germany

Tools and methods

I use Canon EOS 400D + 50mm f/1.8 or 18-55mm/55-200mm, Canon AE-1 + 50mm f/1.8
Tripod, remote control and natural lighting.

The relationship with own body

This is something I cannot express in words and most of all don't want to. There are hints concerning this question in several of my photos and those contain everything I want people to know about that topic.

Behind the scenes

I'm still going to school, but I had my a-levels this year. I only have an oral examination left and will be done with school on june 26. I know that I want to go to uni next year, but I yet have to decide on a study course.

Idea of self-expression

Primarily, I want to retain what I am like for myself to see in the future. I like the fact that I can go back to the photos I took a year from today and I connect memories with them. What I enjoy most about self portraiture is that it helps me to cope with those situations and feelings.

What led you to the world of Internet?

I first started using the internet regularly when I found a forum about my favourite books. I started talking to the people there and even met some of them in real life . One day a girl posted a link to Deviantart and I decided to become a member.

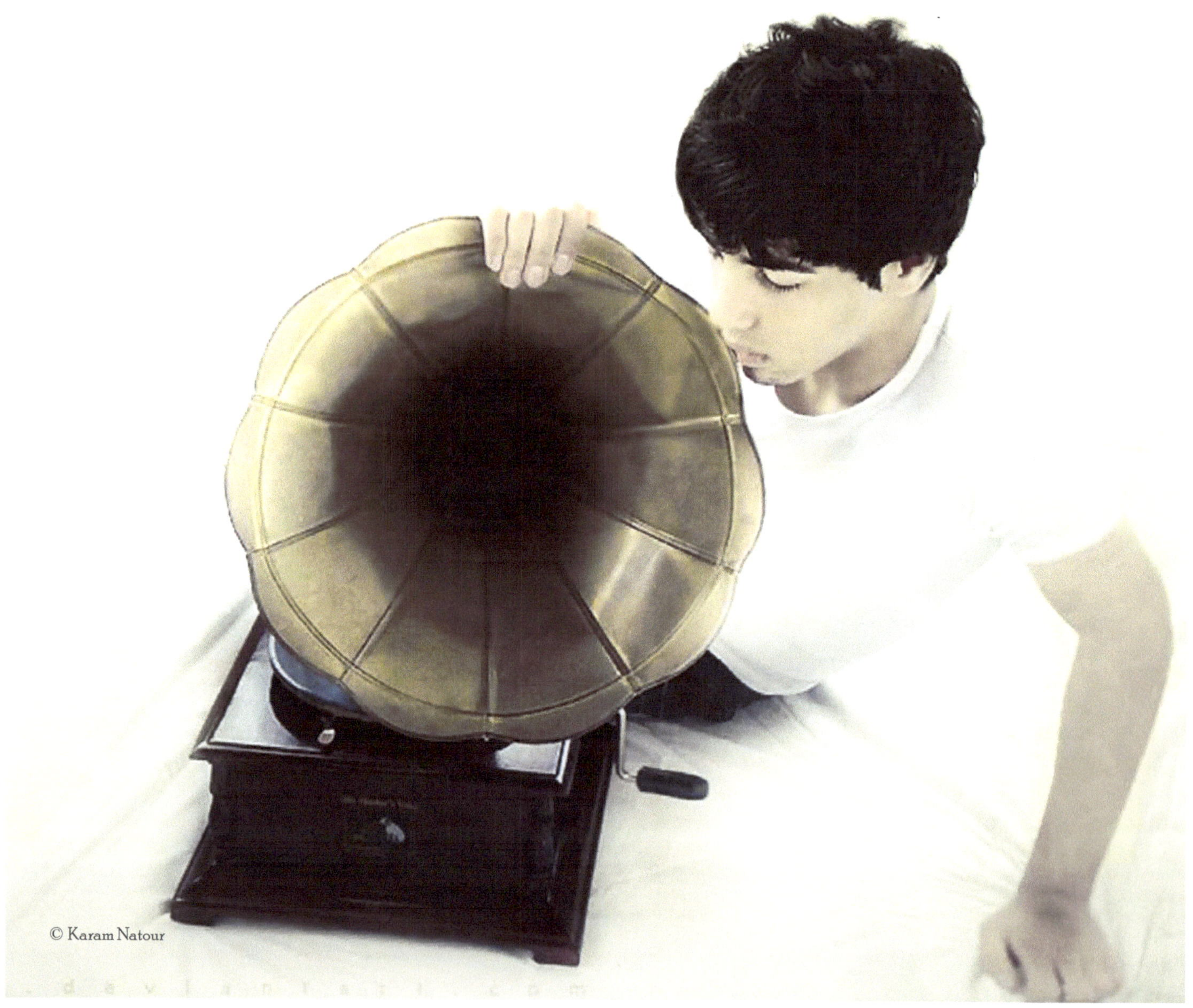
© Karam Natour

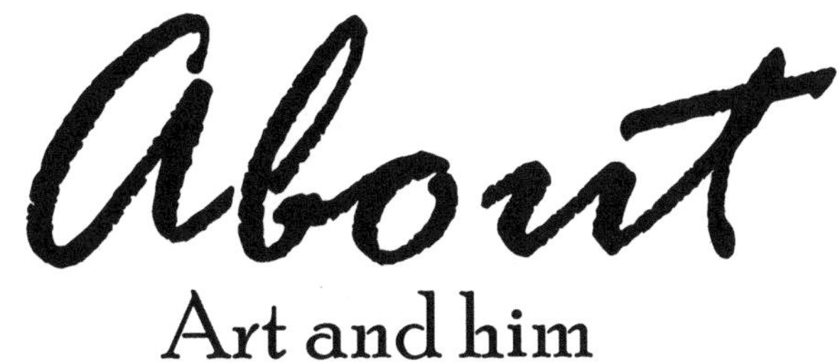

Art and him

Karam Natour

Shefa-Amr, Israel

Tools and methods

My cameras: Canon Digital Rebel XTi and Olympus OM-1 with Canon EF 50mm f/1.4 and Canon EF-S 18-55mm f/3.5 lenses. Tripod Manfrotto 055xb Tripod + 804RC2 Head
Software: Adobe Photoshop CS 4 and Adobe Lightroom 3.

The relationship with own body

I would say that my relationship with my body is quite intense. It shifts the inner me to a different form in which noticeable details could be shown more clearly. It's like my body is the reflection of my thoughts and the echoes of my fears. A mysterious kind of relationship that still feels far to obvious.

Behind the scenes

Currently, I am on the edge of graduating from high school. Apart from that, I volunteer whenever I get the chance to, at different kinds of associations and organizations. Faith and volunteering have a great compact in my life. Making people happy is and will be one of my great goals in life. Additionally, I try to drag myself in the faith-topic, it is warming, it makes me feel different.

Idea of self-expression

1) Showing aspects of your being that you don't usually see 2) Turning concepts of yourself into a photograph that holds emotions 3) Spreading your thoughts in a different ways that gives you satisfaction

What led you to the world of Internet?

I found a place I could express myself in, internet fills a lot of my gaps.

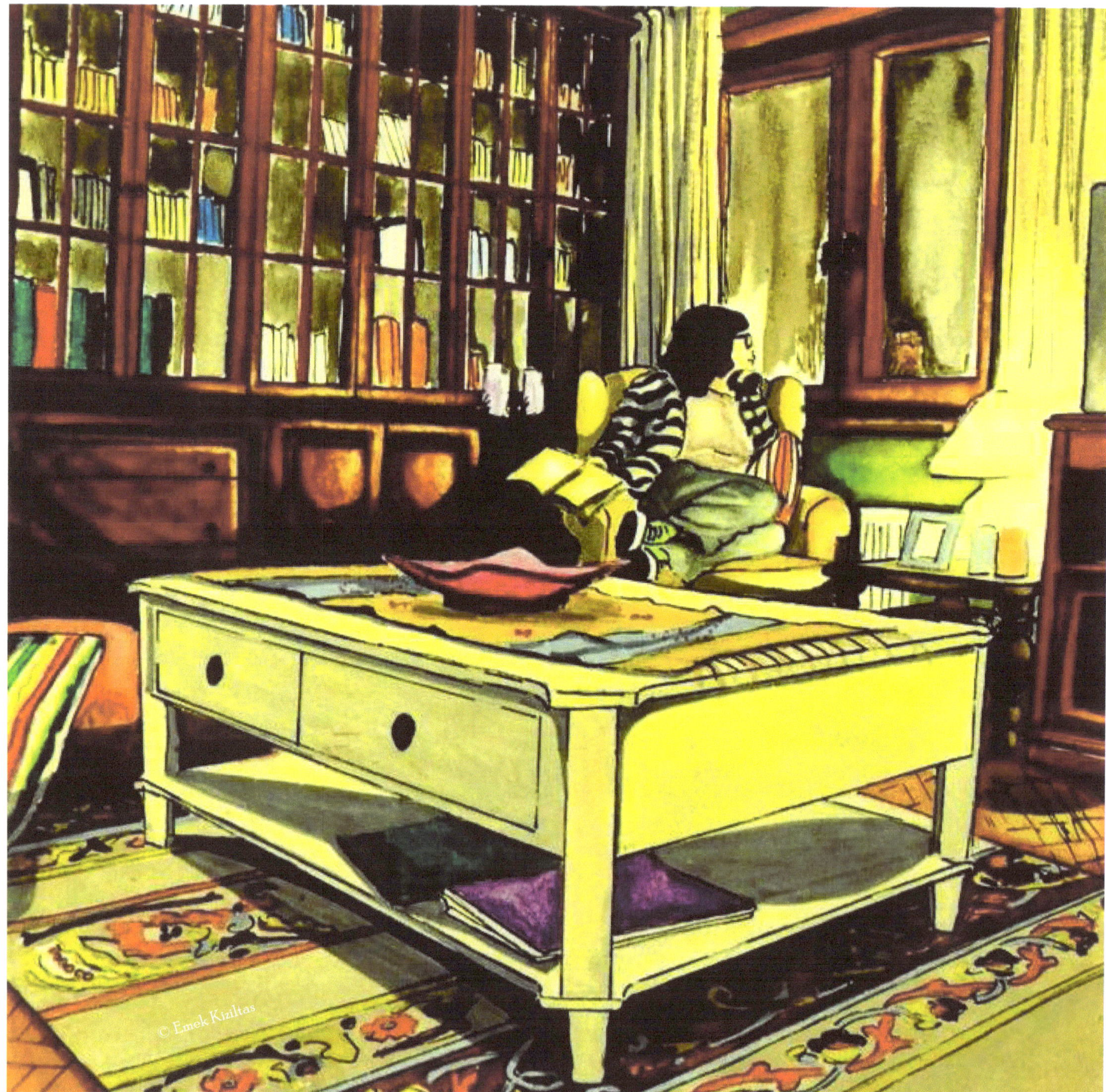
© Emek Kiziltas

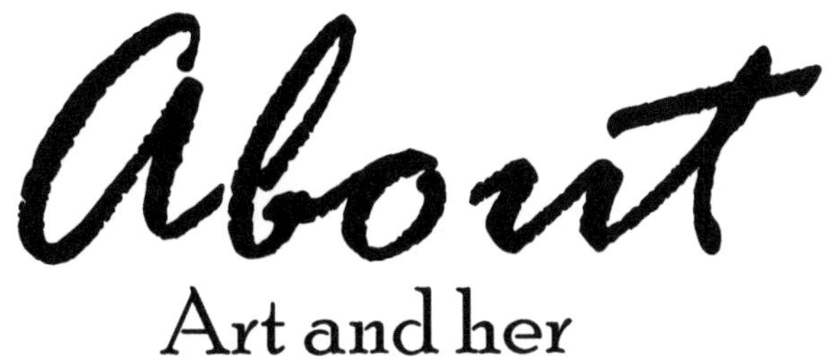

Art and her

Emek Kiziltas

Istanbul, Turkey

Tools and methods

Mostly I prefer to use watercolour, acrylic colour, markers and graphic pens. Even though I do illustrations on any kind of paper, at the same time I try to keep in relation between myself and classical methods with using oil and canvas.

The relationship with own body

I consider this as an experience. The body is developing with experiences as long as we live. and accumulates a huge potential with itself. That is way I am still at the stage to dig out and identify my body.

Behind the scenes

There is a very line between ideas and real life. I am studying at combined arts in Arts and Designs Facility in Turkey. I spend my spare time with reading and following up the new ideas about arts and designs.

Idea of self-expression

Even though I express myself with my favourite tools which are colours and papers, just drawing, painting and giving forms is not enough. Talking, writing, yelling and performing provide me the fluxional way I prefer instead of being stable.

What led your to the world of internet?

There was no internet when I was born. I don't know if it is a good thing but I am older than internet! I think it is useful as long as I want to share my works and meet people all over the world. I don't have any bad experience for the present. I am a member of one or two popular websites and I follow some others about art and design.

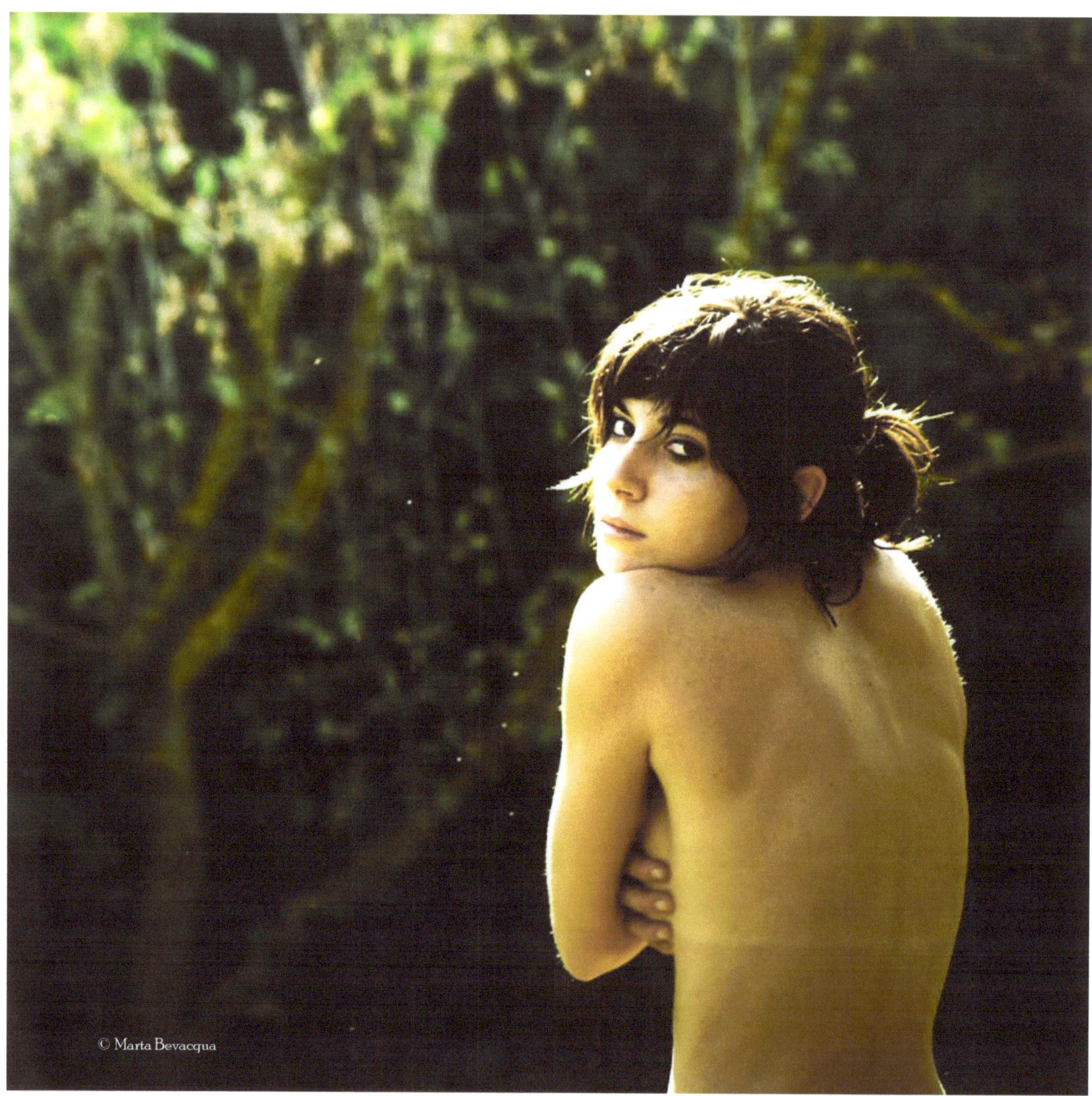

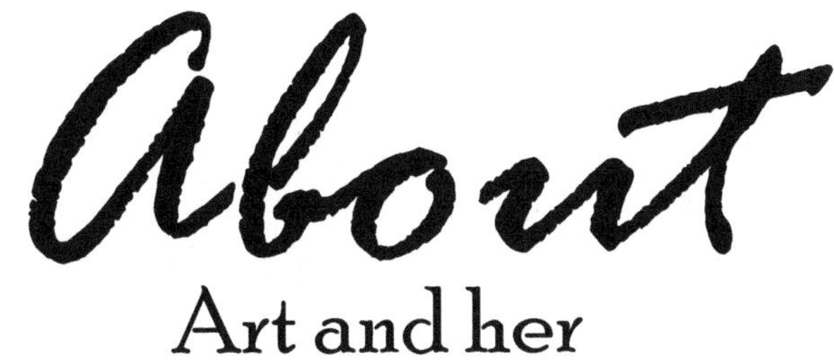

Art and her

MOTH ART - Marta Bevacqua photos

Rome, Italy

Tools and methods

I used to have a Sony alpha 100, then it was stolen from me, so now I used an Olympus. Now I'm planning to buy a new camera. In my self-portraits I usually use the self-timer, but in some rare cases I ask someone to take the shot under my direction..

The relationship with own body

I have a quite good relationship with my body. I'm also quite shy, so I don't like so much being noticed and wear simple dresses. There are times when I want to show my body and I feel really appreciated in some ways and it makes me feel well with myself and my body. These days it happens quite often.

Behind the scenes

I went to university where I was really unsure how to choose between Physics and Italian and foreign literature. Then I gave up everything: I simply understood how much I love photography and decided this will be my future. It was very difficult to me: I had to convince everyone that I could do this and live on it.

What led you to the world of Internet?

I entered the world of photography through Internet and it was love on the first sight when I browsed photography oriented websites. Now Internet is an important thing to be visible and it is easy to find me and my work.

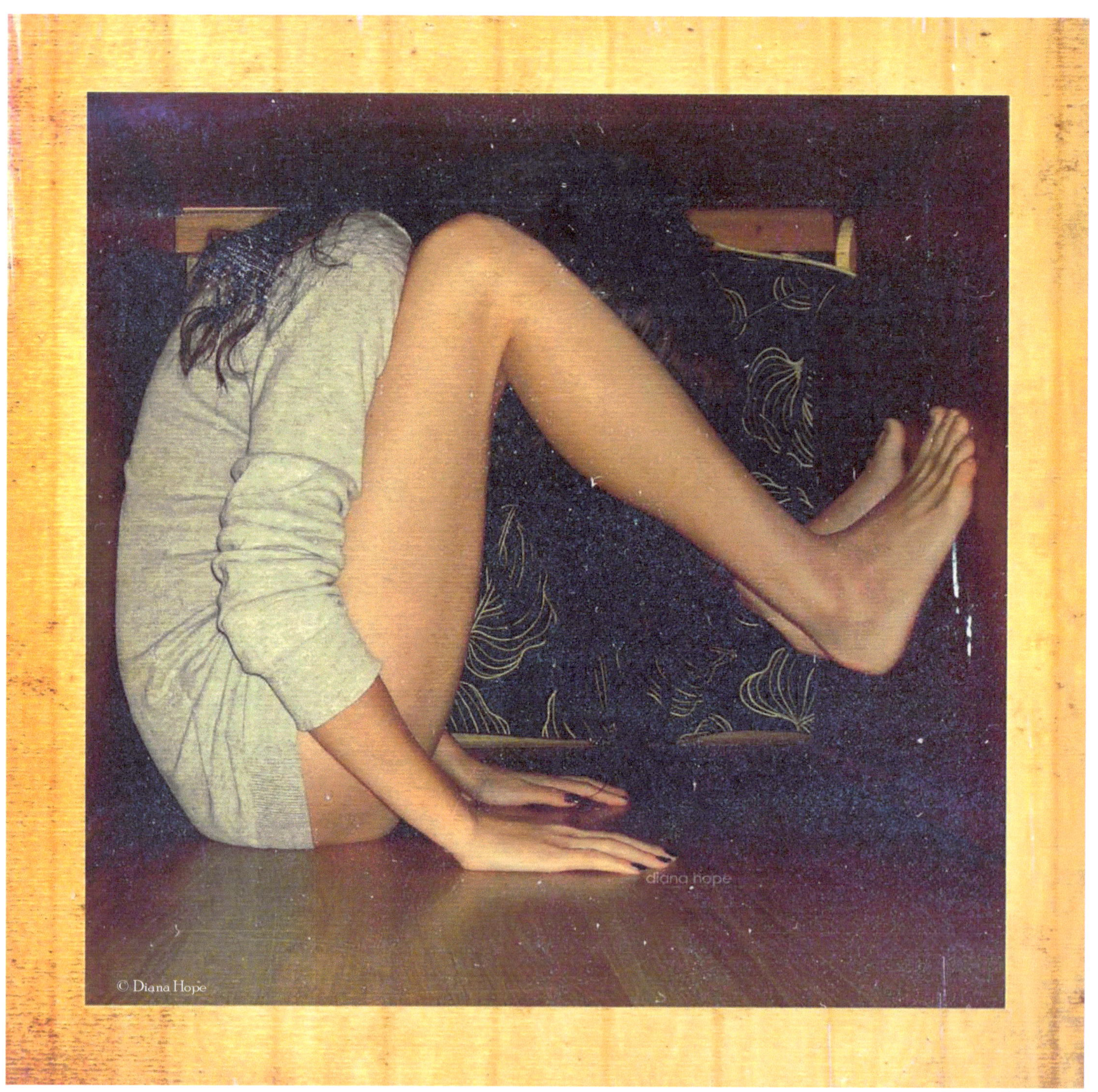
diana hope
© Diana Hope

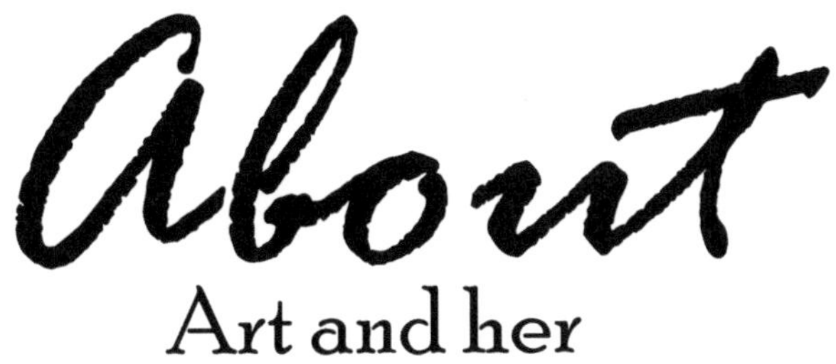

Art and her

Diana Hope

Moscow, Russia

Tools and methods

My tools are Sony DSC-W90 and Adobe Photoshop CS4 Windows.

The relationship with own body

No comment.

Behind the scenes

I graduated from Art school and college with excellent grades, specialising as an animator.
Currently I am working in a school with children teaching them to draw cartoons.
I'm planning to study in the British Higher School of Design to get a prestigious education and go abroad to work in the field of art and advertising in 2011.

Idea of self-expression

I'm an artist. What can I say? I'm just different and to be honest:
I'm not a model nor a photographer.
I'm an amateur. Still I'm just an artist.
But I'd like to learn professional photography and I'd like to stay as some kind of model, if I am found suitable for the purpose.

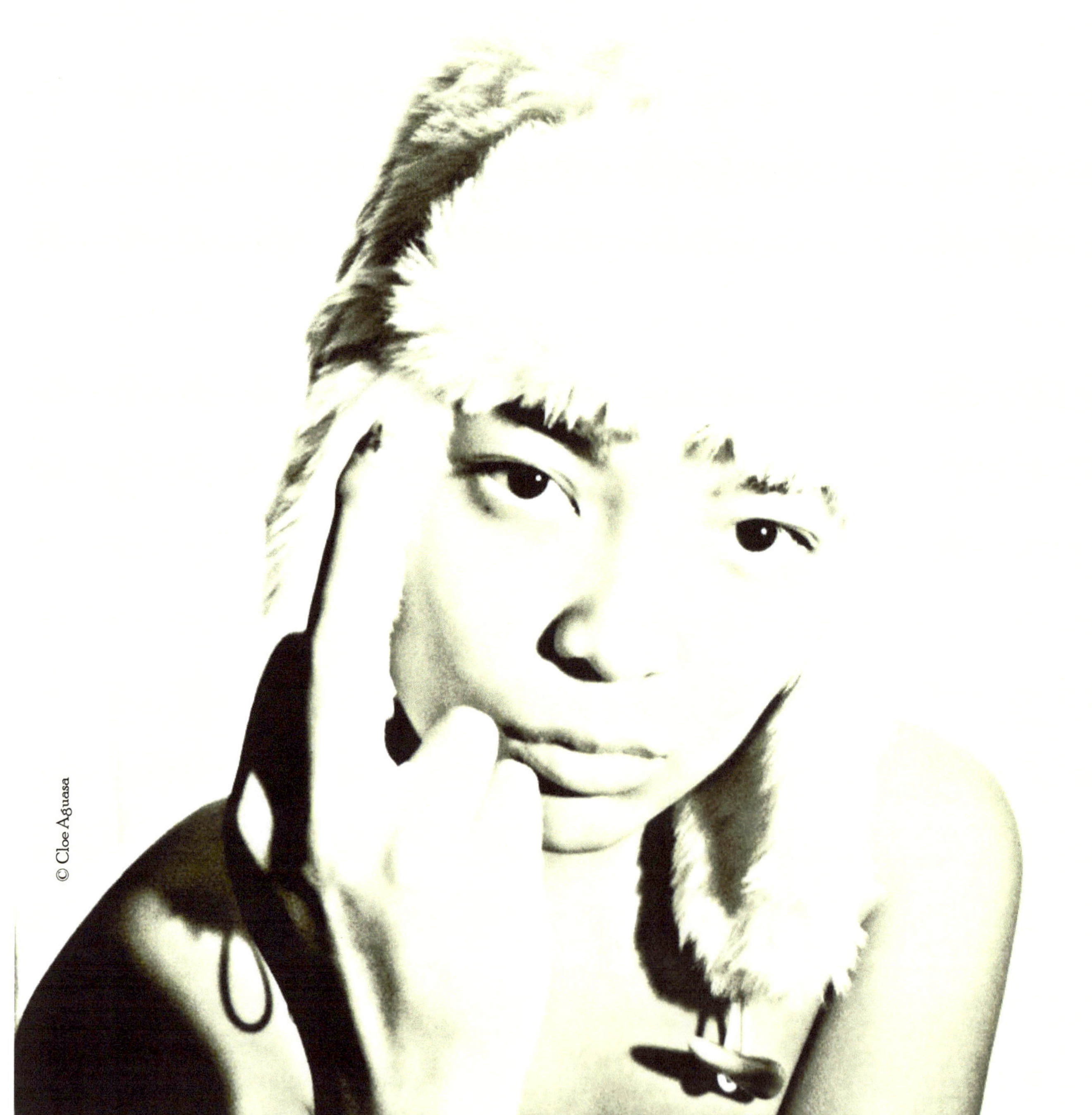

© Cloe Aguasa

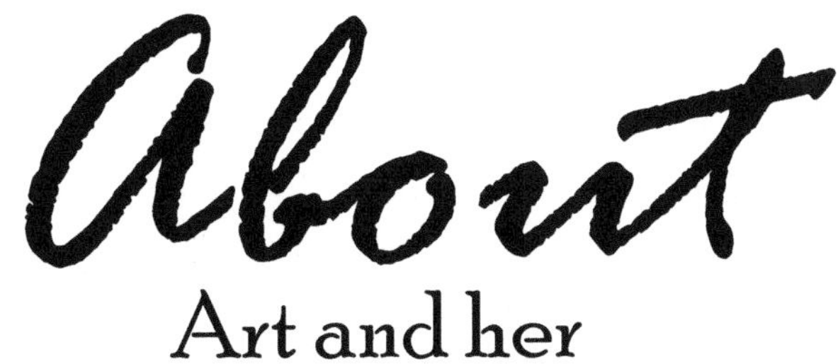

Art and her

Chloe Aguasa

Vancouver, Canada

Tools and methods

A Nikon camera.

The relationship with own body

I love my body, no matter how it looks.
My body is a temple, a piece of art.

Behind the scenes

In real life, I am a student.
The busiest thing these days for me are cultural matters.

Idea of self-expression

Art is the best way to express one's self, and it doesn't really matter in which form it's in.

What led you to the world of Internet?

I found it out of curiosity.
The good thing is that I can share my art to the wide spread media through Internet.
The bad thing is exploitation.

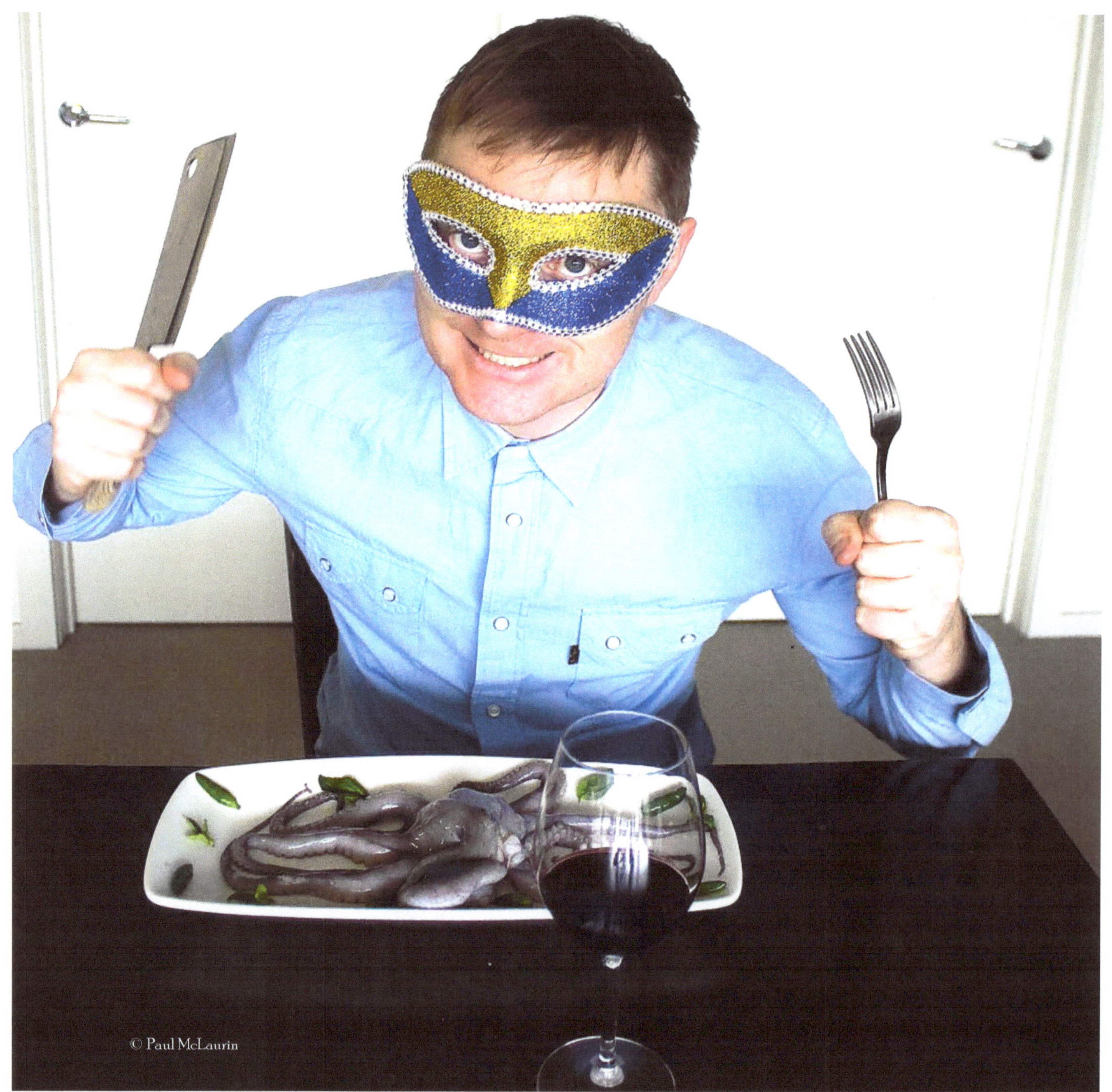
© Paul McLaurin

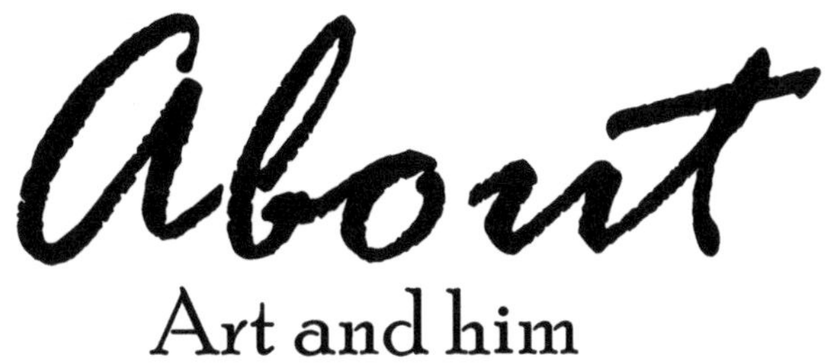

Art and him

Paul McLaurin

Melbourne, Australia

Tools and methods

My tools are DSLR (Canon 7D) and a variety of different light sources and props to add some theatricality to my work. For post-processing I use Photoshop CS5.

The relationship with own body

When you use your body as an artistic resource it's very difficult not to be self-conscious, especially if part of your work requires you to be vulnerable, and to pitch yourself against other people's subjectivity.
As I get older, I understand more about what it takes to maintain it, and to care for it to make sure that it's a part of my life that facilitates the experiences I want, rather than limits them.

Behind the scenes

I am a photography student and I also work in Human Resources.

Idea of self-expression

I use photography to express my world view –I feel that self-portraiture gives me the permission to explore a theatricality that is otherwise absent in my life.

What led you to the world of Internet?

I think the Internet is the biggest advancement in human history, it has turned a vast and isolated planet into a village and the exchange of ideas has become exponentially more rapid. It is a peerless consciousness raising medium, and the potential for user generated content means that there is an endless feed of media that is produced not for commercial gain but for its own sake – that's so powerful.

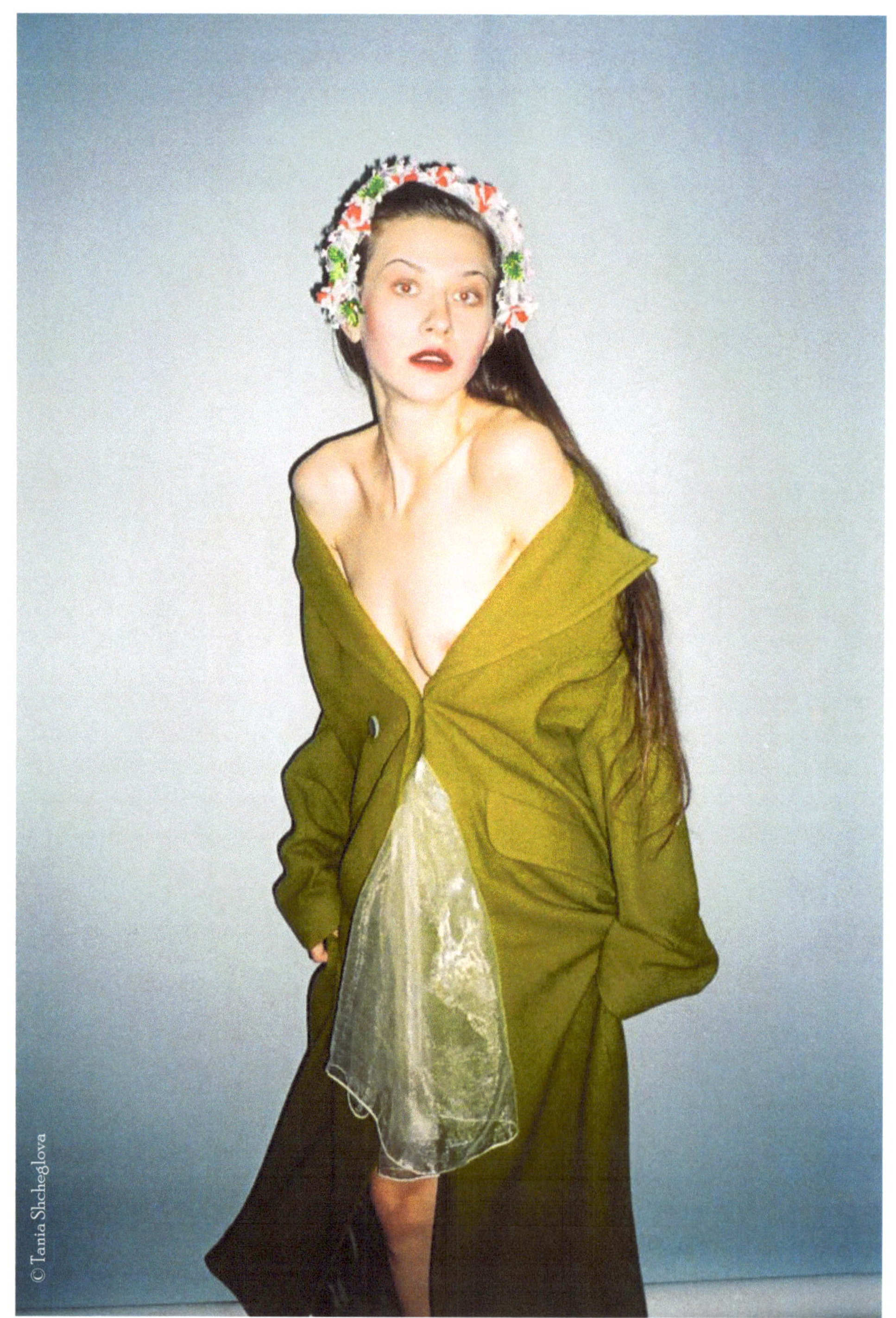

© Tania Shcheglova

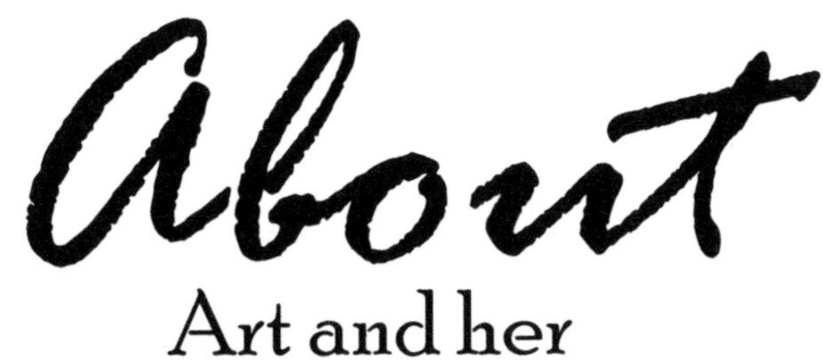

About

Art and her

Tania Shcheglova

Synchrodogs.com, Ukraine

Tools and methods

Cameras and non-existing clothes.

The relationship with own body

Slavery and freedom all together.

Behind the scenes

I shoot photos and draw in my secret small book. In a week there are total of two days that I spend in a train, and 10h in a day I use for sleeping, 5h for talking, another 5h for thinking, 2 hours for eating, 1h for walking. It sounds busy, but there is still 1h of reserve time.

Idea of self-expression

You don't have to take it too seriously. Just use any place that inspires you, any material that can be transformed into clothes, any piece of string that can become accessory. There is no need to go out of your skin to make it look glamorous. Just let the mess come out!

What led you to the world of Internet?

Long live The Internet! Space bless all the bloggers! I would rather not be neutral, as for this moment it's the only way for somebody to get to know about us (me and my boy Roma as we usually take the photos together). I try not to think of somebody stealing my ideas, and then writing his or her name under it. That would take too much of my hyper energy. However, I try to trust people and even though they stole something I'd do nothing bad, maybe just put a curse on their bones.

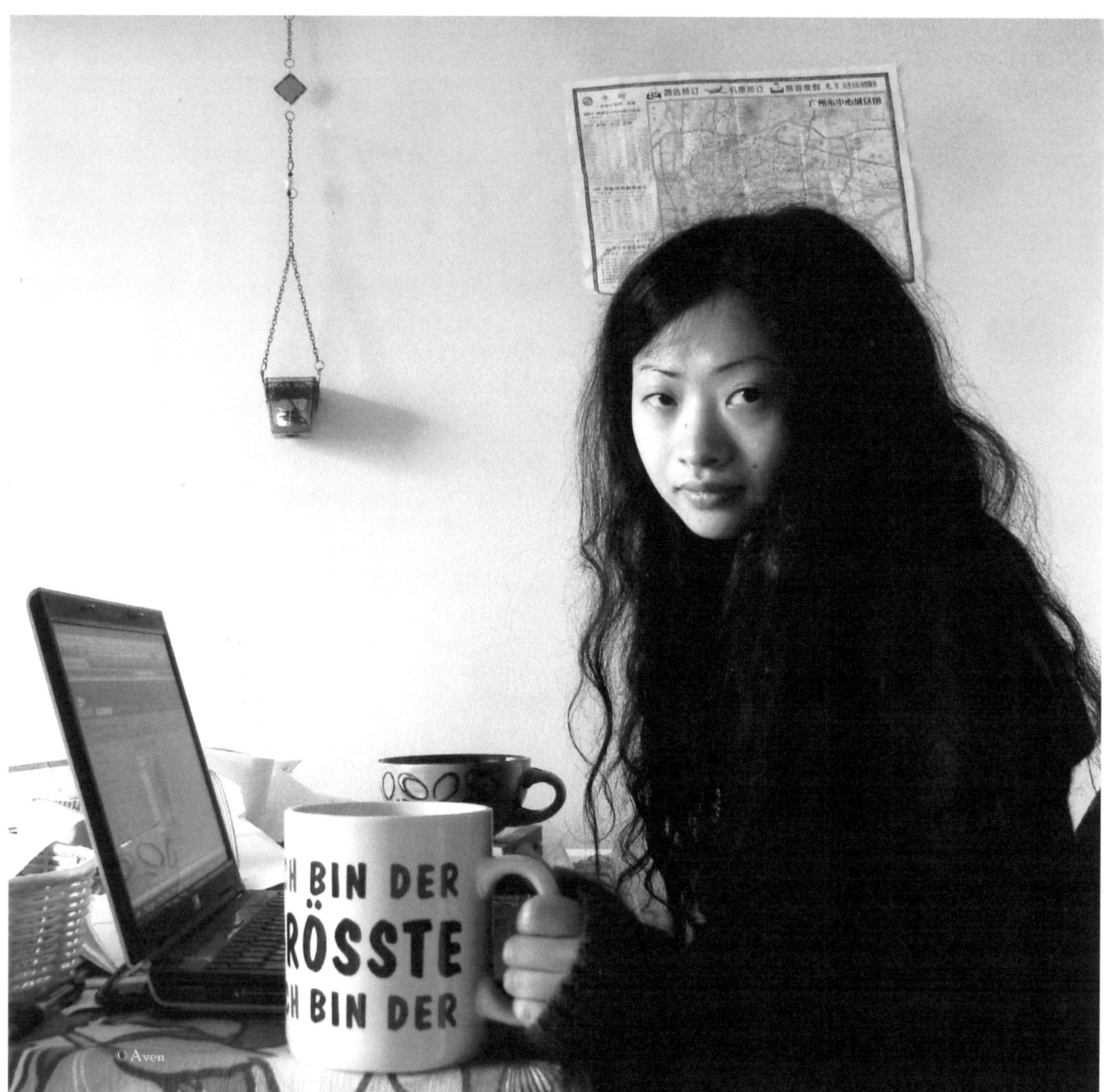
CH BIN DER
RÖSSTE
CH BIN DER

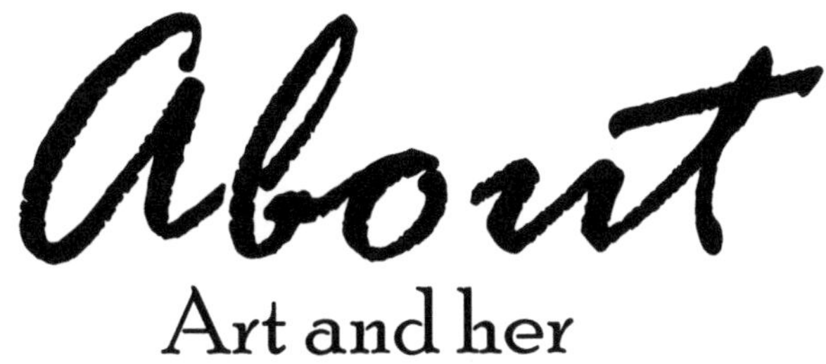

Art and her

Aven

GuangDong, China

Tools and methods

Buckets, chairs, tables, bottles.. Whatever that can hold my camera with a timer. The rest needs sometimes more, sometimes less imagination.

The relationship with own body

I am not always comfortable with it, it's something between ackward and „just-do-it". I need verbal comminucation to tell whether someone who observes my body is admiring or critizising. What I try to remember is: it is my one and only. Don't try to be perfect. Just try to be healthy and clean. Everyone has a chance for that sort of beauty.

Behind the scenes

I am trying to do too many things the same time and to be honest, I'd like to do even more. Besides work and occasional projects I paint, travel, take loads of pictures while travelling, plan studying further and try out the funny or weird ideas that come to my mind.

Idea of self-expression

I prefer things that doesn't need to be clean or tidy, but have dignity.

What led you to the world of Internet?

My first computer was brought all the way from Australia and it was quite a puzzle to install an Internet access. Internet is my everyday companion. It delivers my news, my entertainment, and I am available when people need to reach me. It is a channel that can cause misunderstandings and a lot of trouble, but I see it's benefits weight more on the scale.

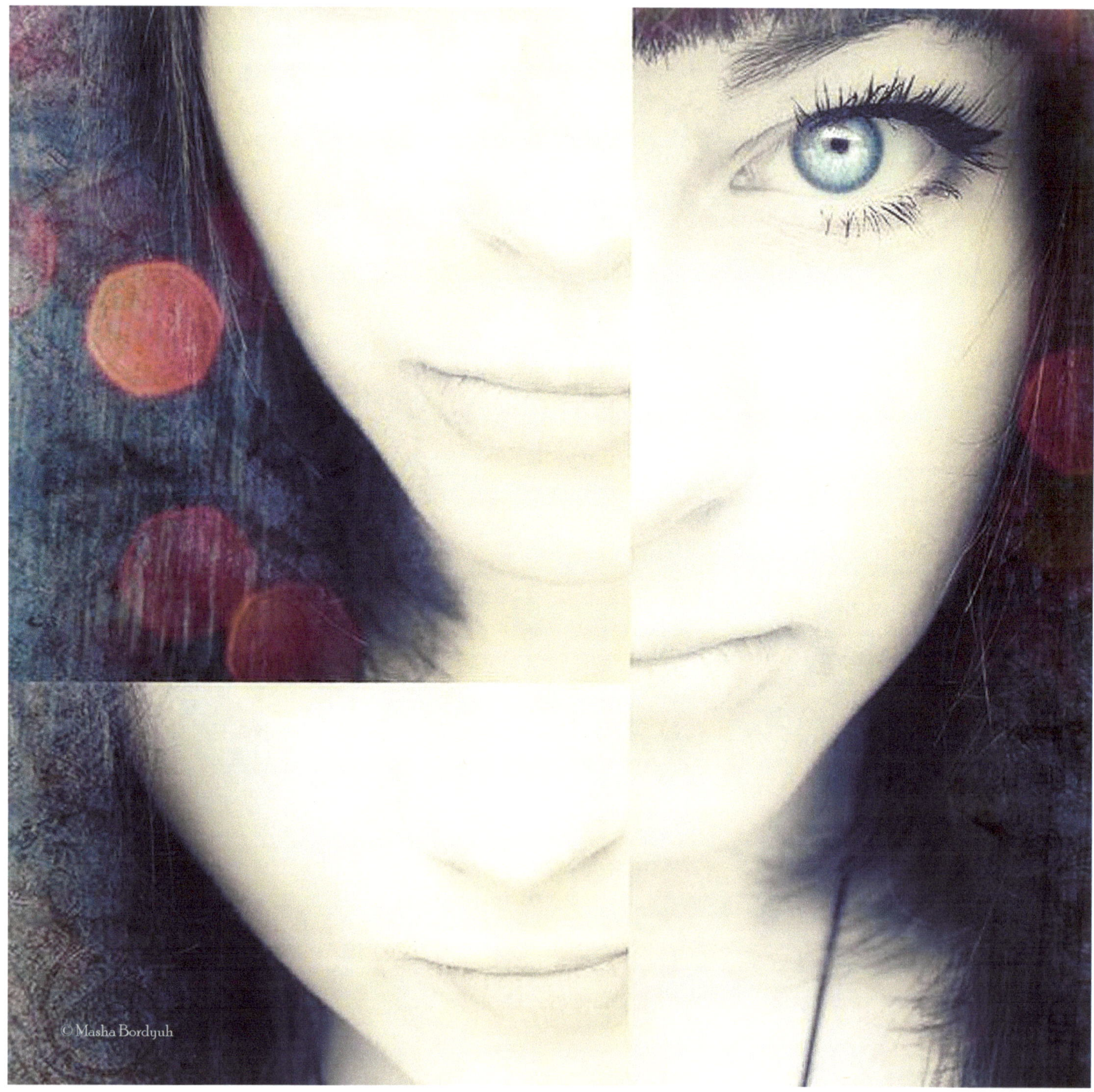
©Masha Bordyuh

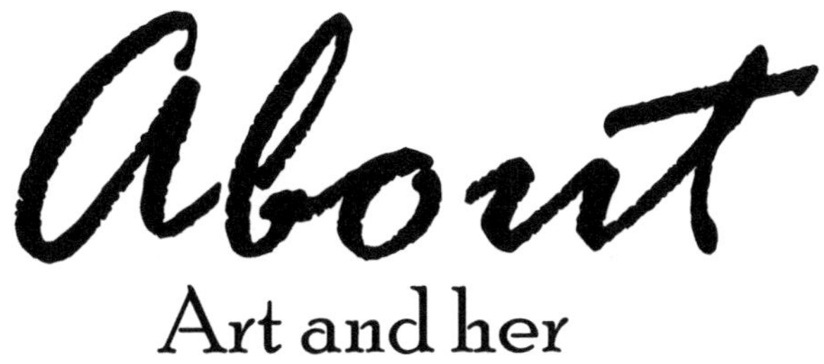

Art and her

Masha Bordyuh

Kiev, Ukraine

Tools and methods

Nikon D40, Nikon D100, Photoshop CS5, etc.

The relationship with own body

I don't think my body is perfect, but I like some parts of that imperfection. So you could say that it is perfect because of its imperfection.

Behind the scenes

I am studying Japanese, make portraits, read smart books and watch House M.D. Oh! Sometimes I go to the gym, mostly for the fun of it, not to look more muscular! The most important topic for me these days is slightly selfish. Now I'm really searching for the real me, because I don't really know who I am now and where I am going.

Idea of self-expression

I can't express myself with words because of the lack of them, but actually it doesn't really even matter for me how to express myself. Sometimes even just a nice photo works. It all depends on who is watching me, and not everybody is able to see the real me.

What led you to the world of Internet?

Because to me, the Internet is the most convenient way to look for inspiration.

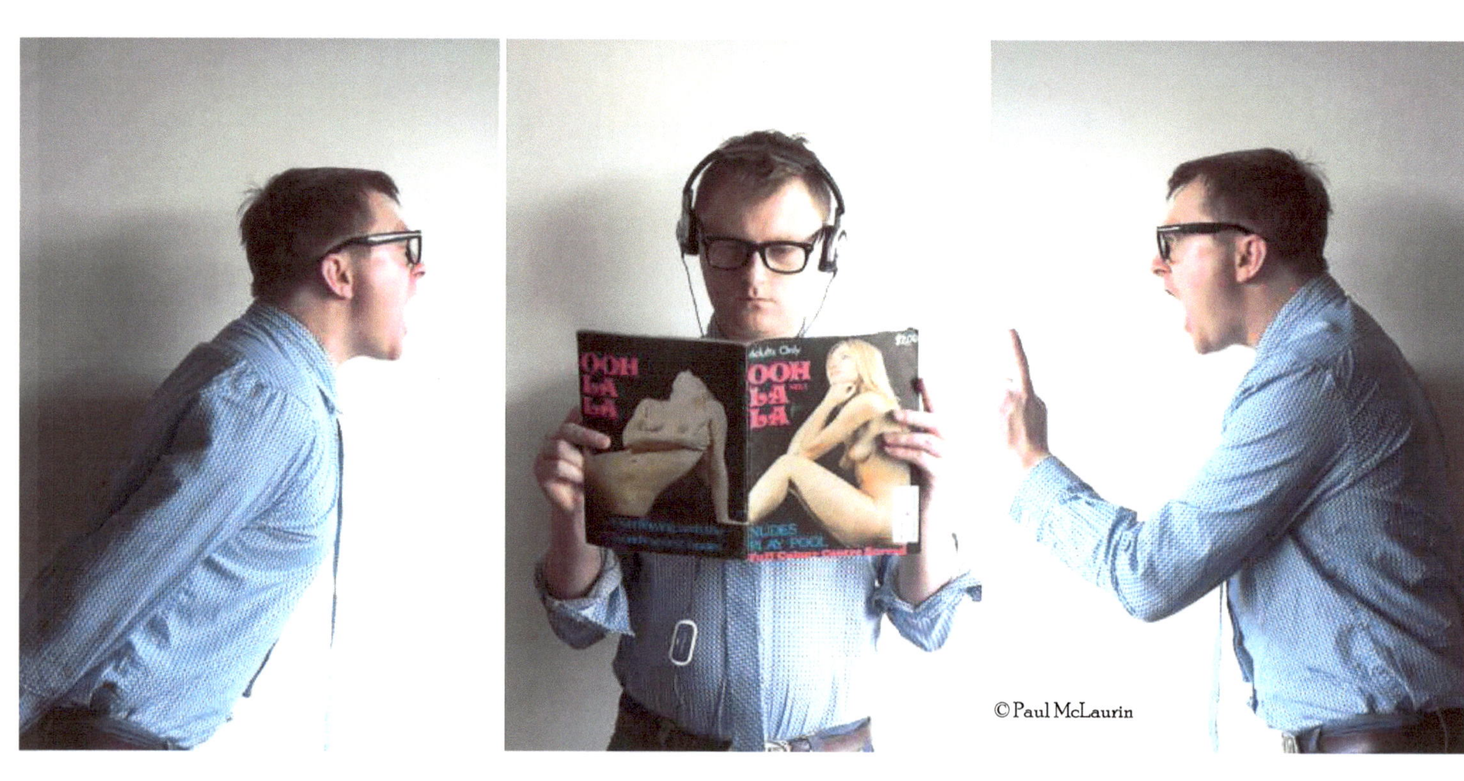
OOH
LA
LA
Adults Only
OOH
LA
LA
NUDES
POOL

THE GALLERY

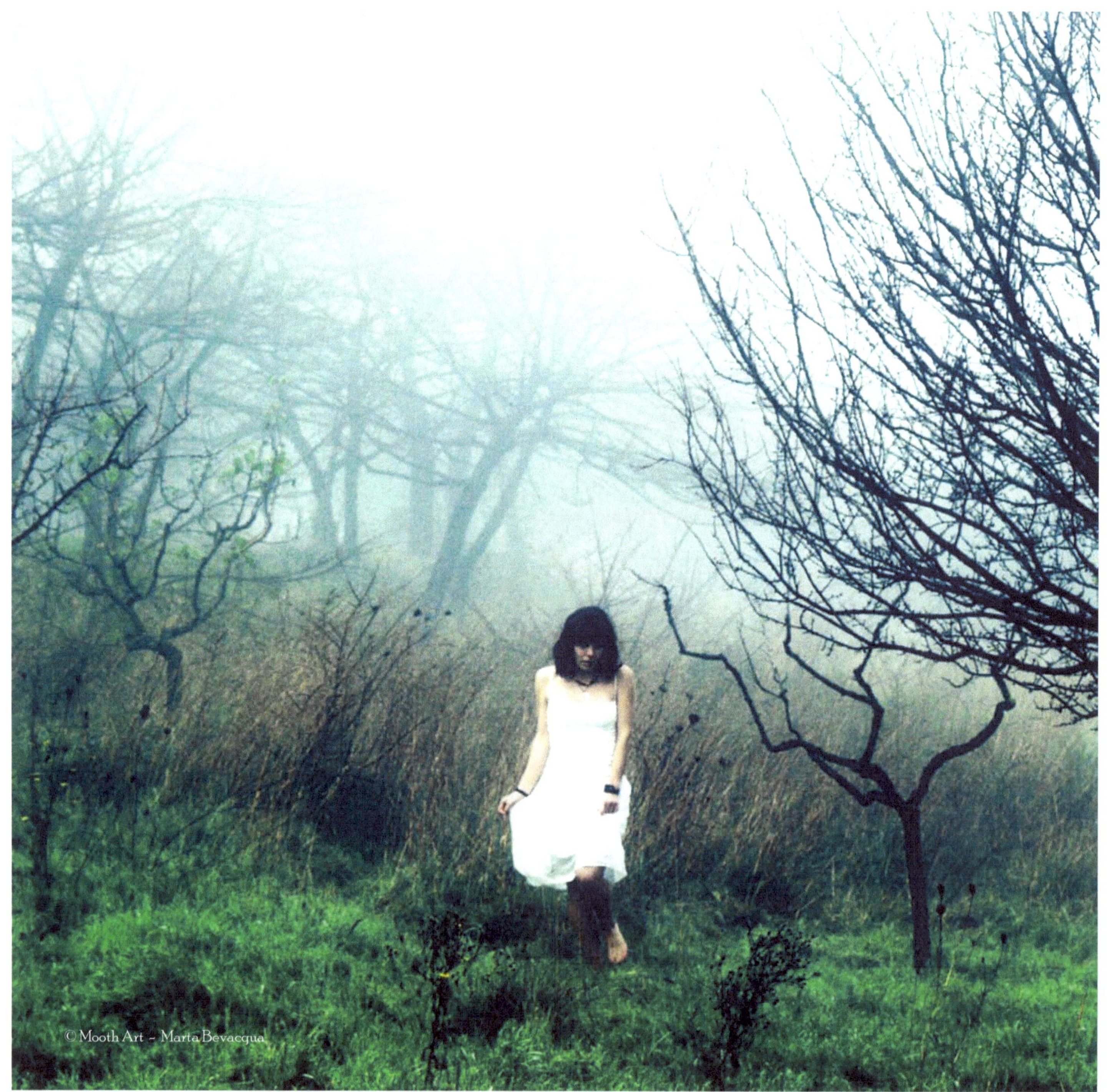
© Mooth Art – Marta Bevacqua

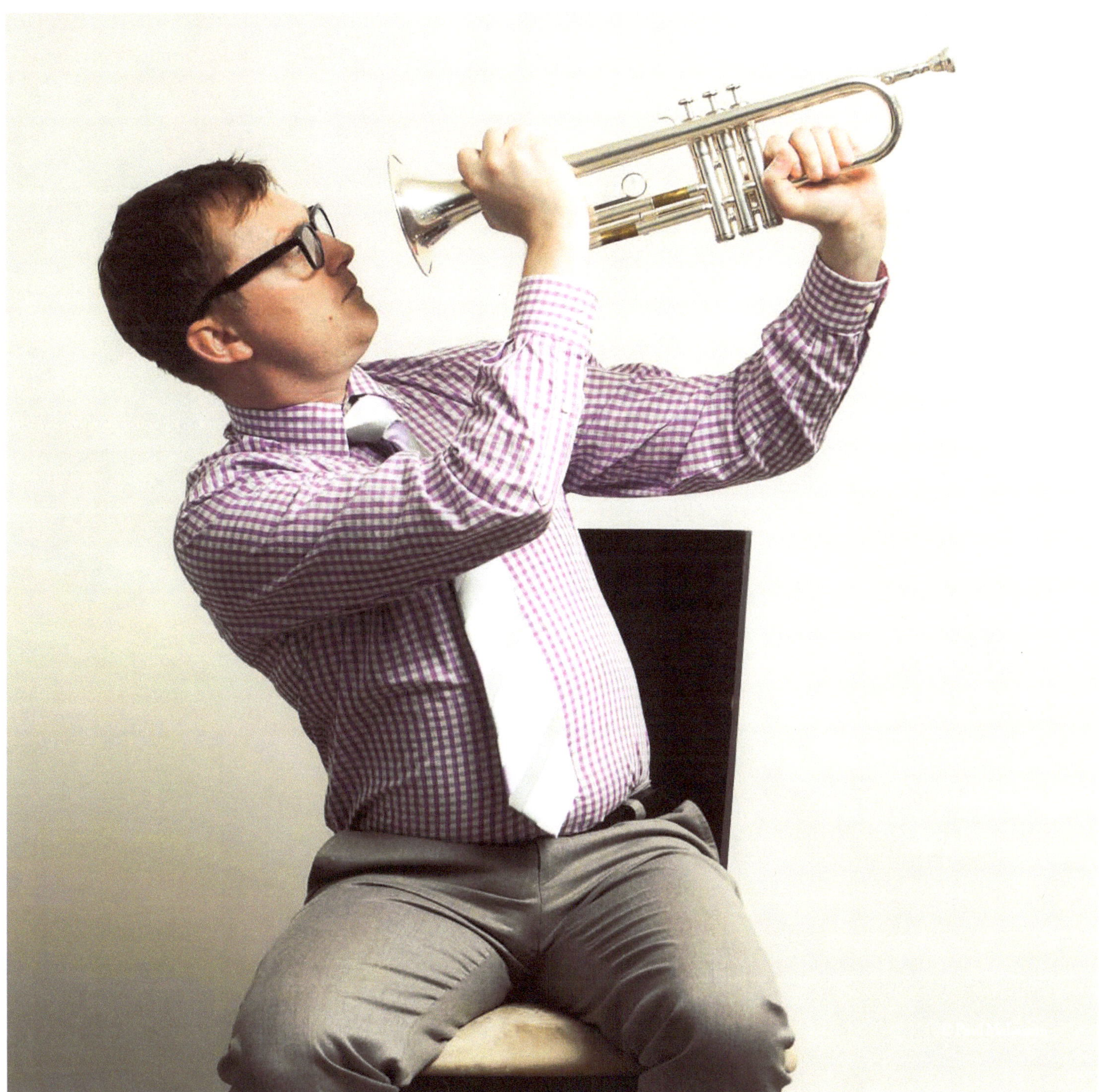

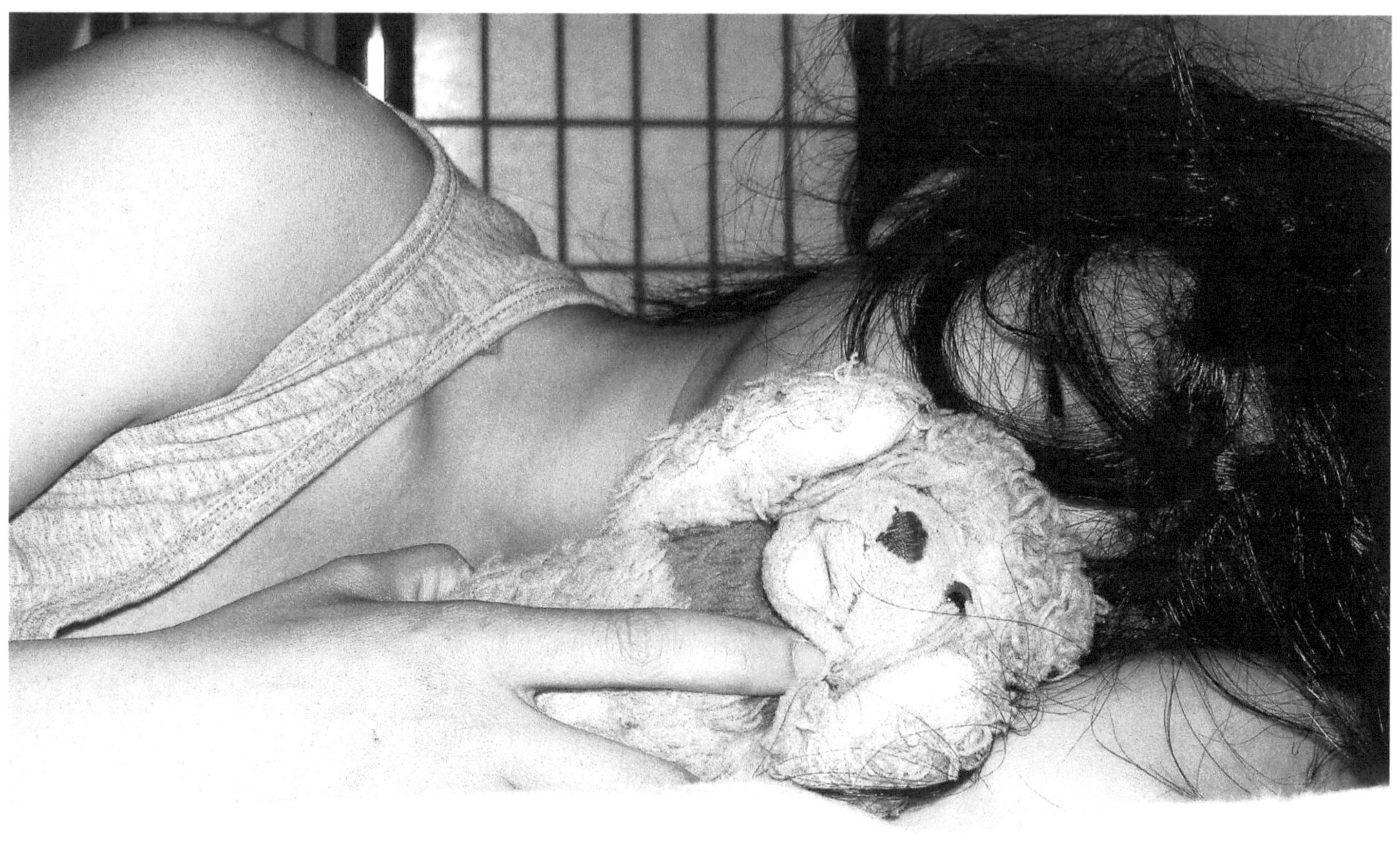

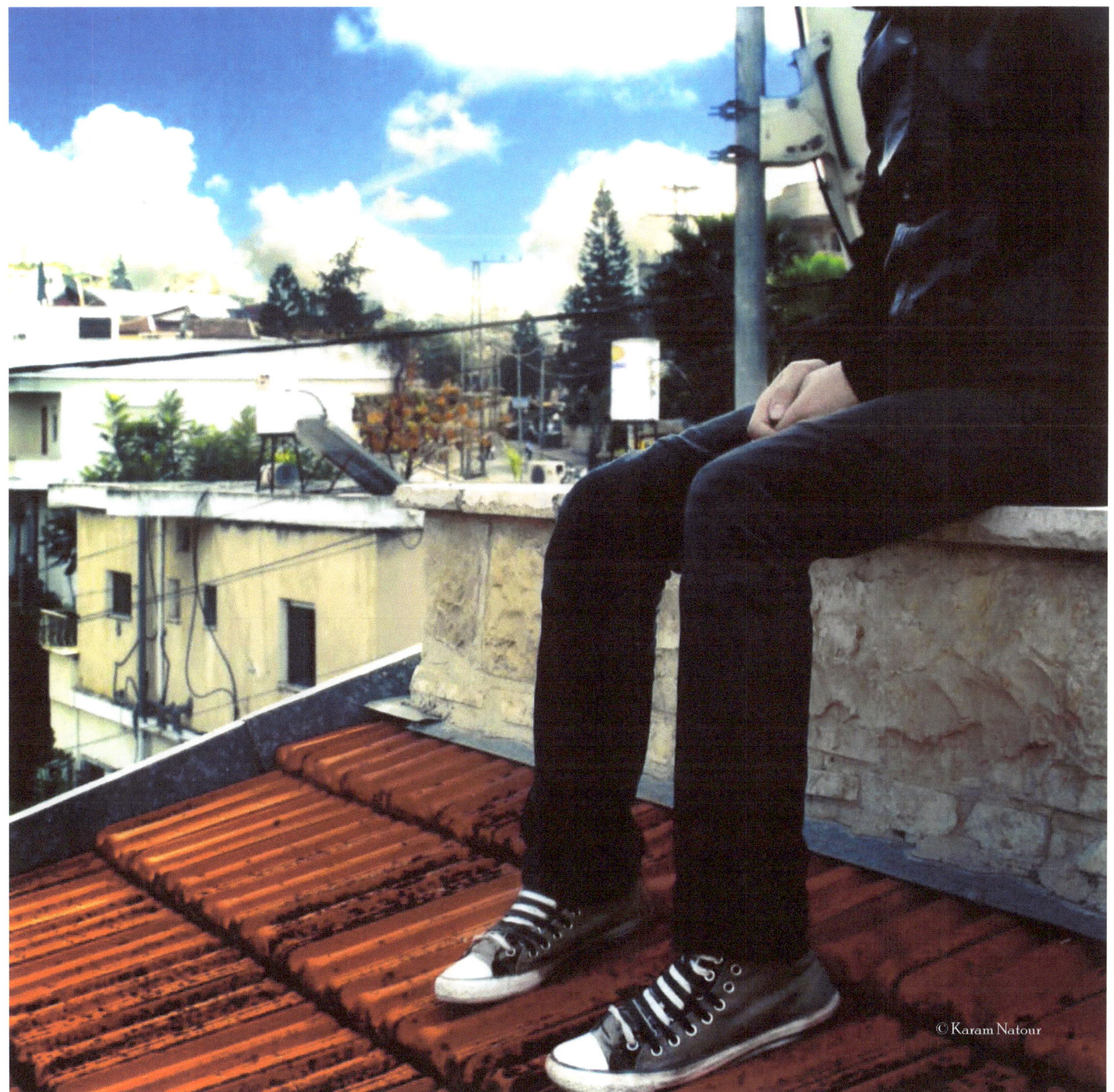
© Karam Natour

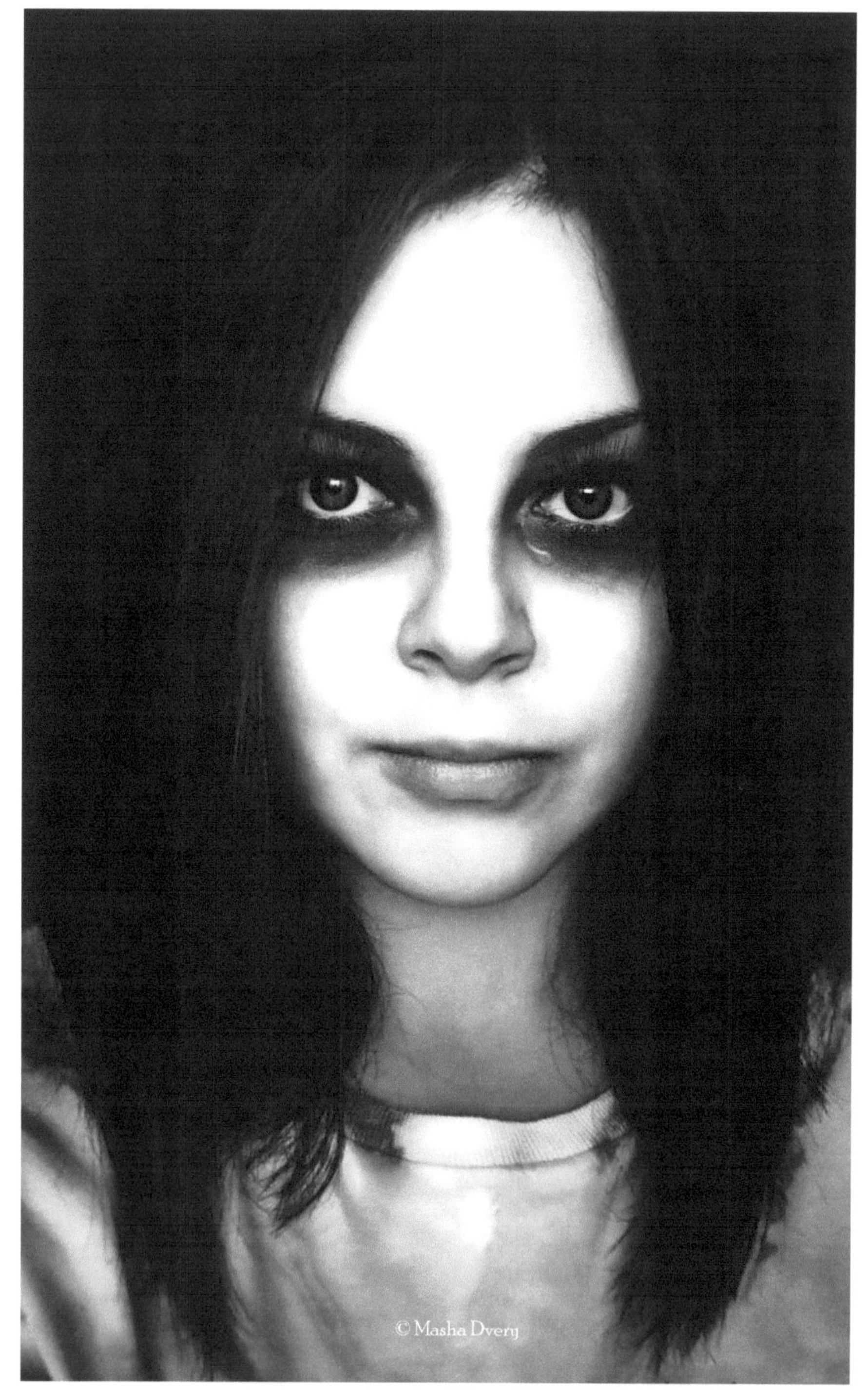
© Masha Dvery

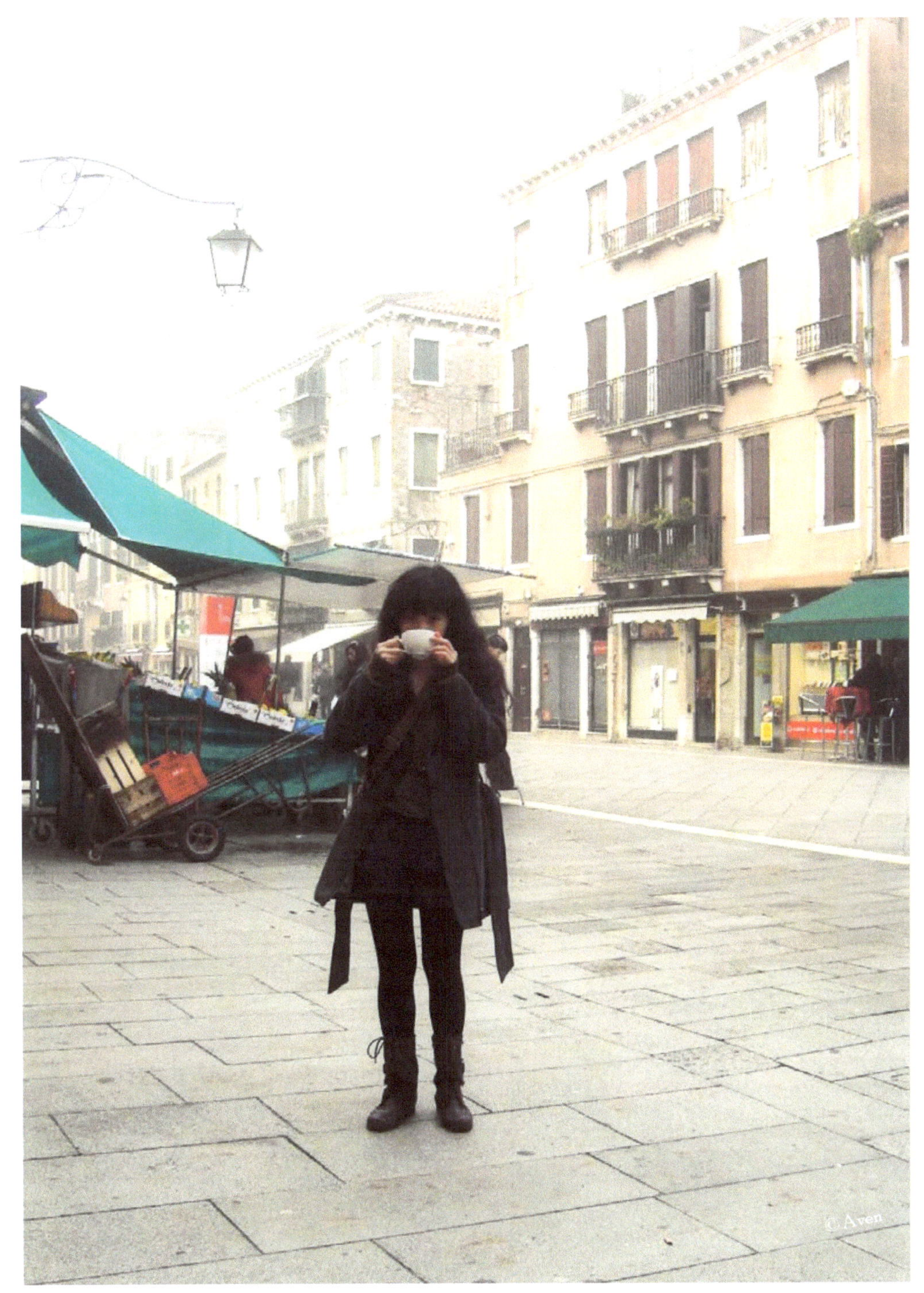
© Aven

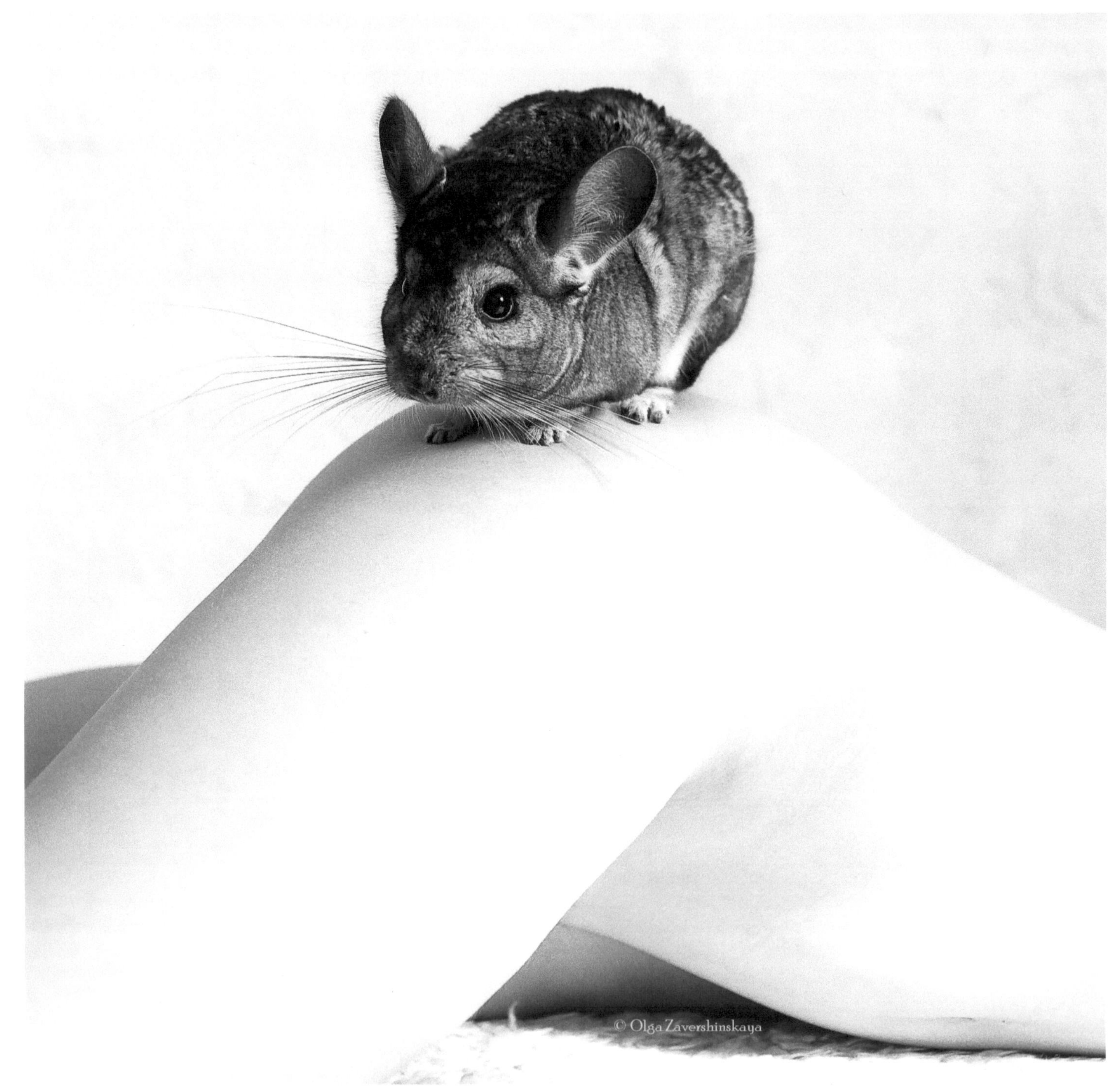
© Olga Zavershinskaya

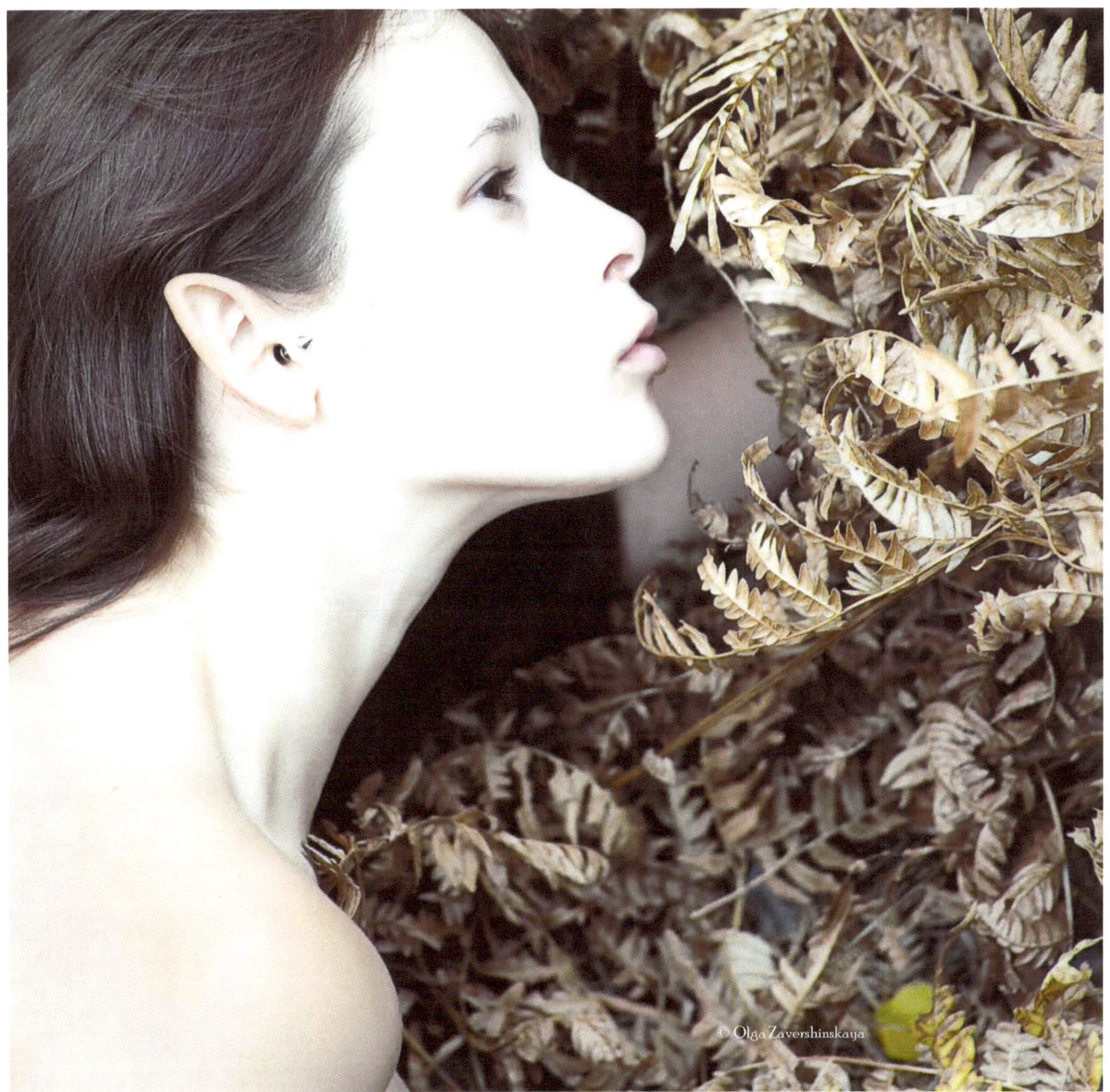
© Olga Zavershinskaya

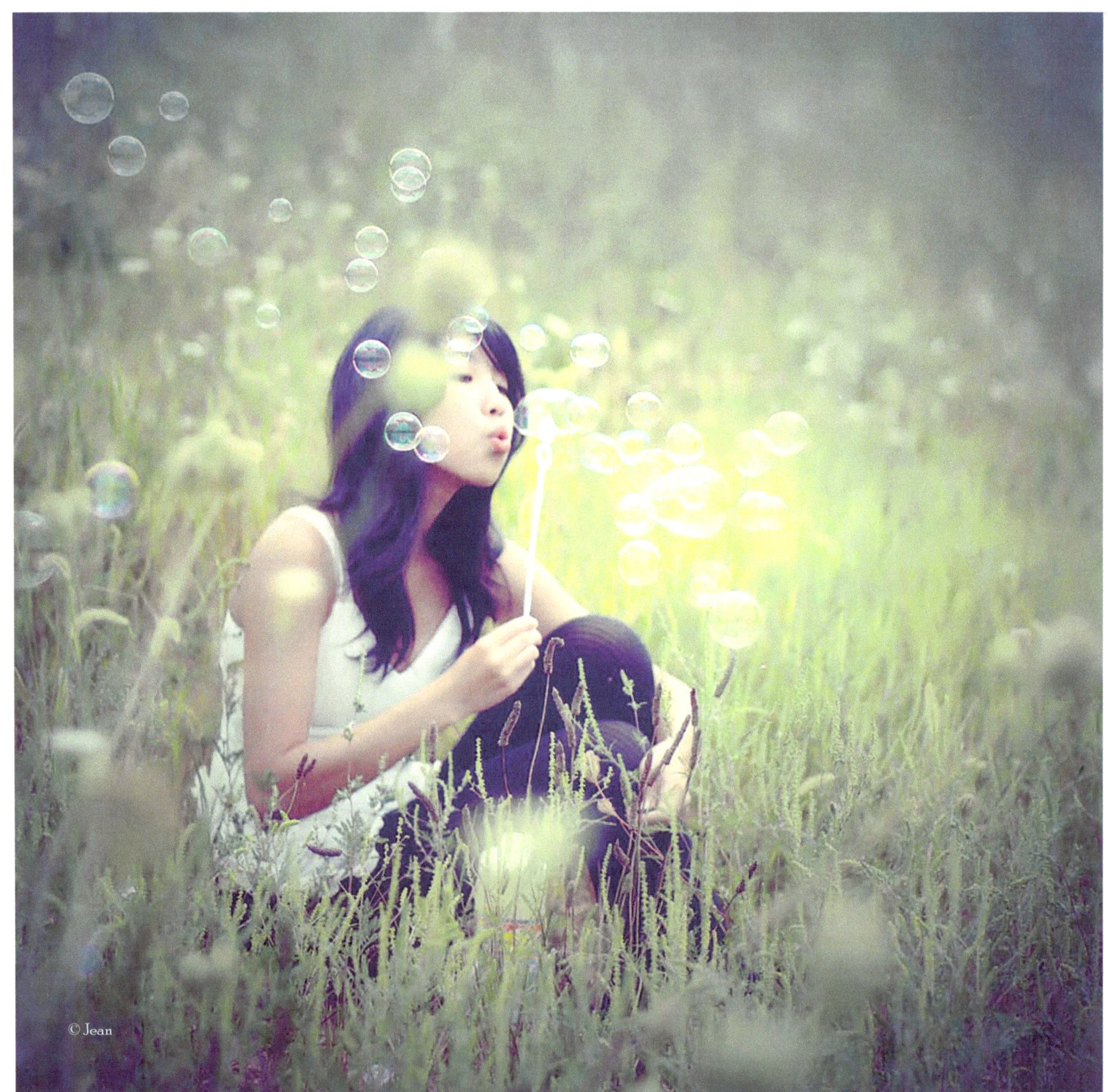
© Jean

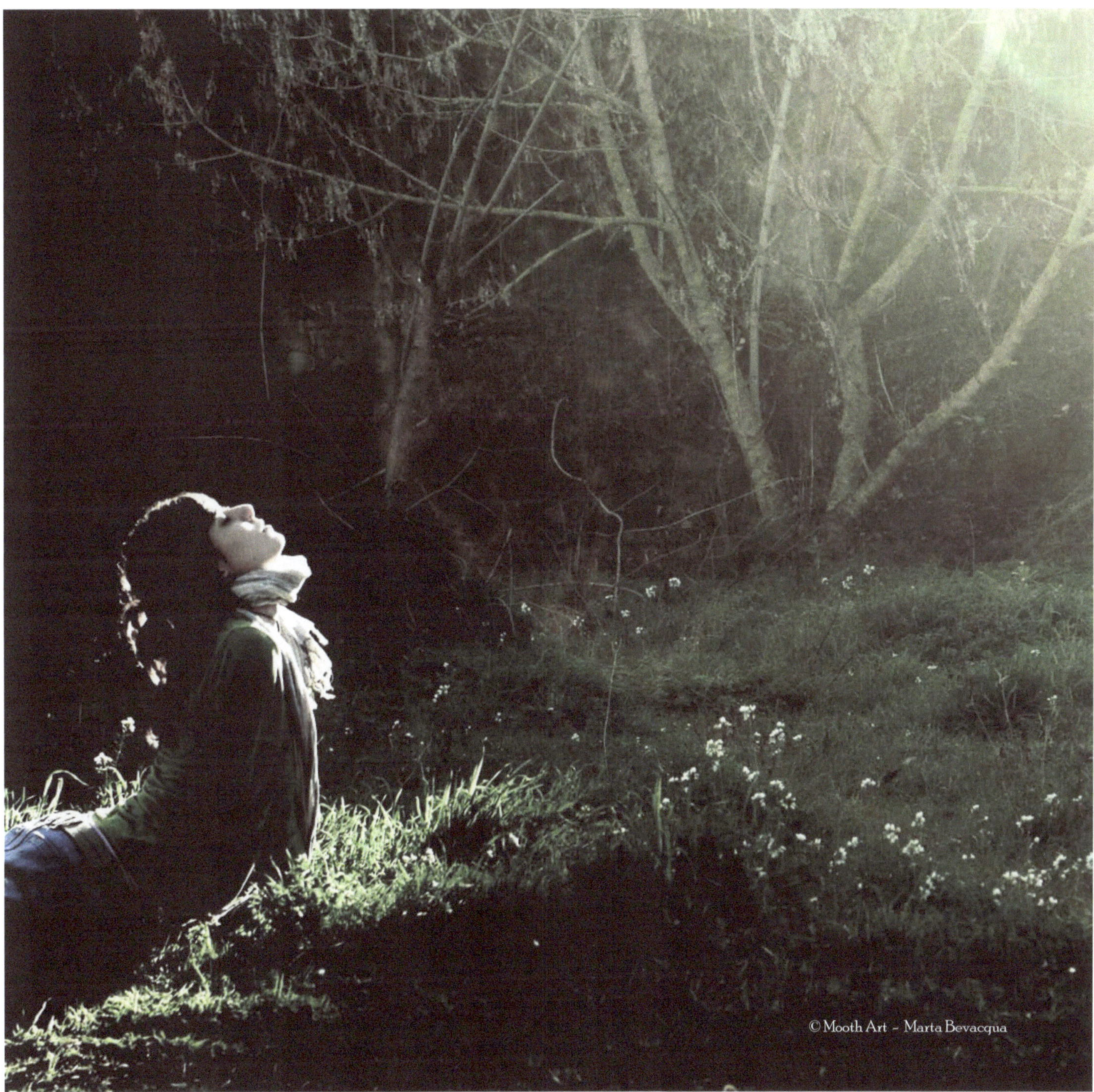
© Mooth Art - Marta Bevacqua

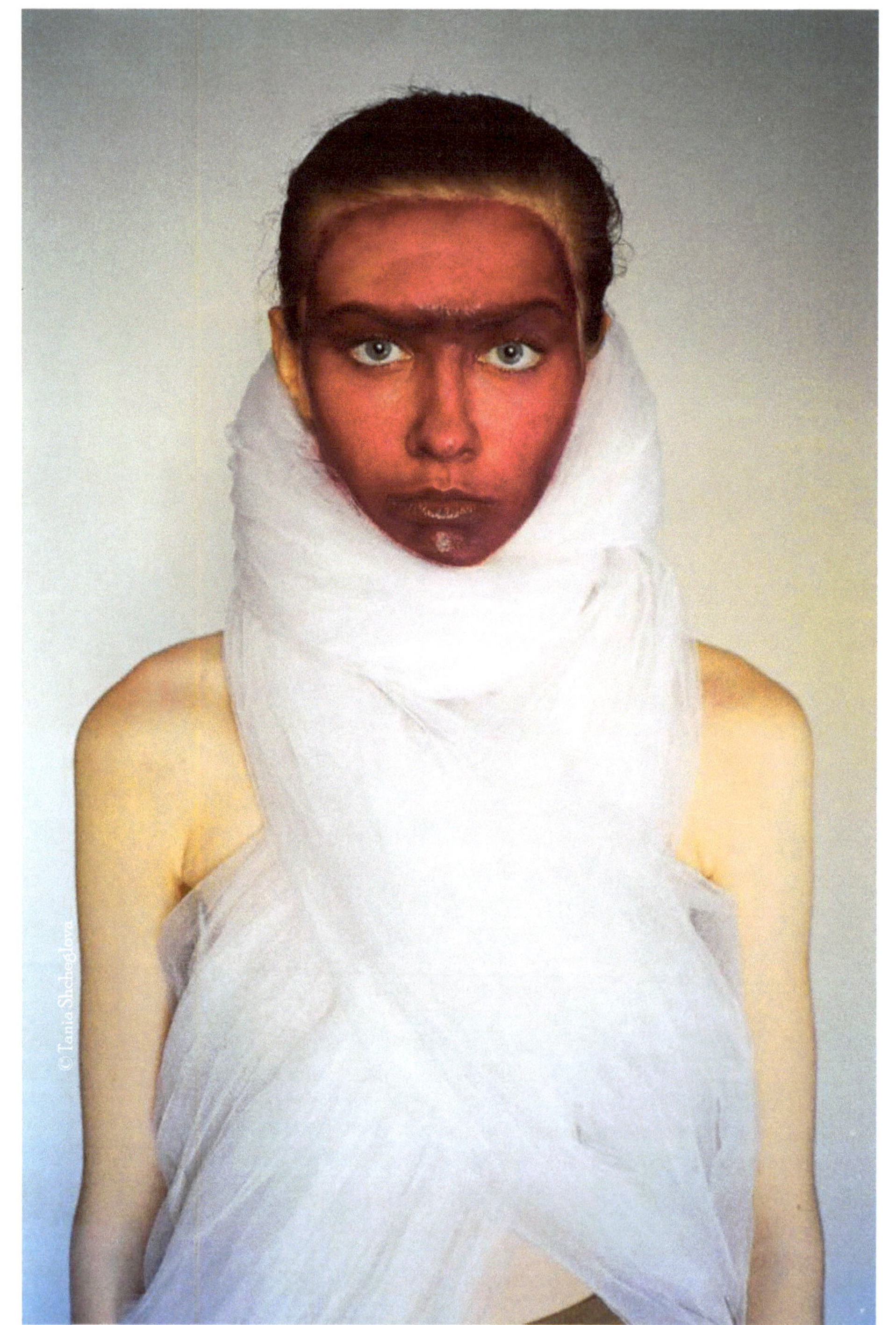

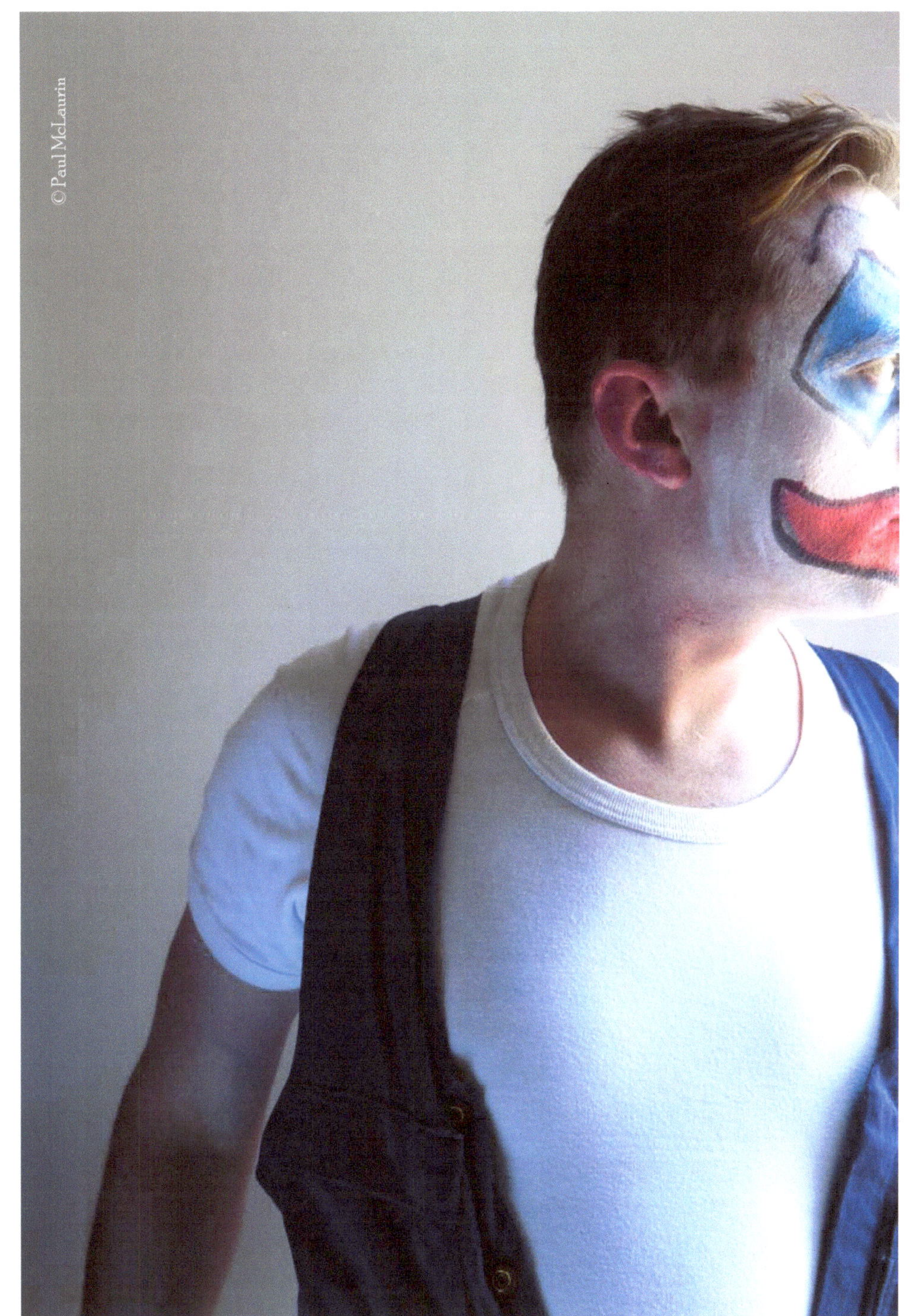
© Paul McLaurin

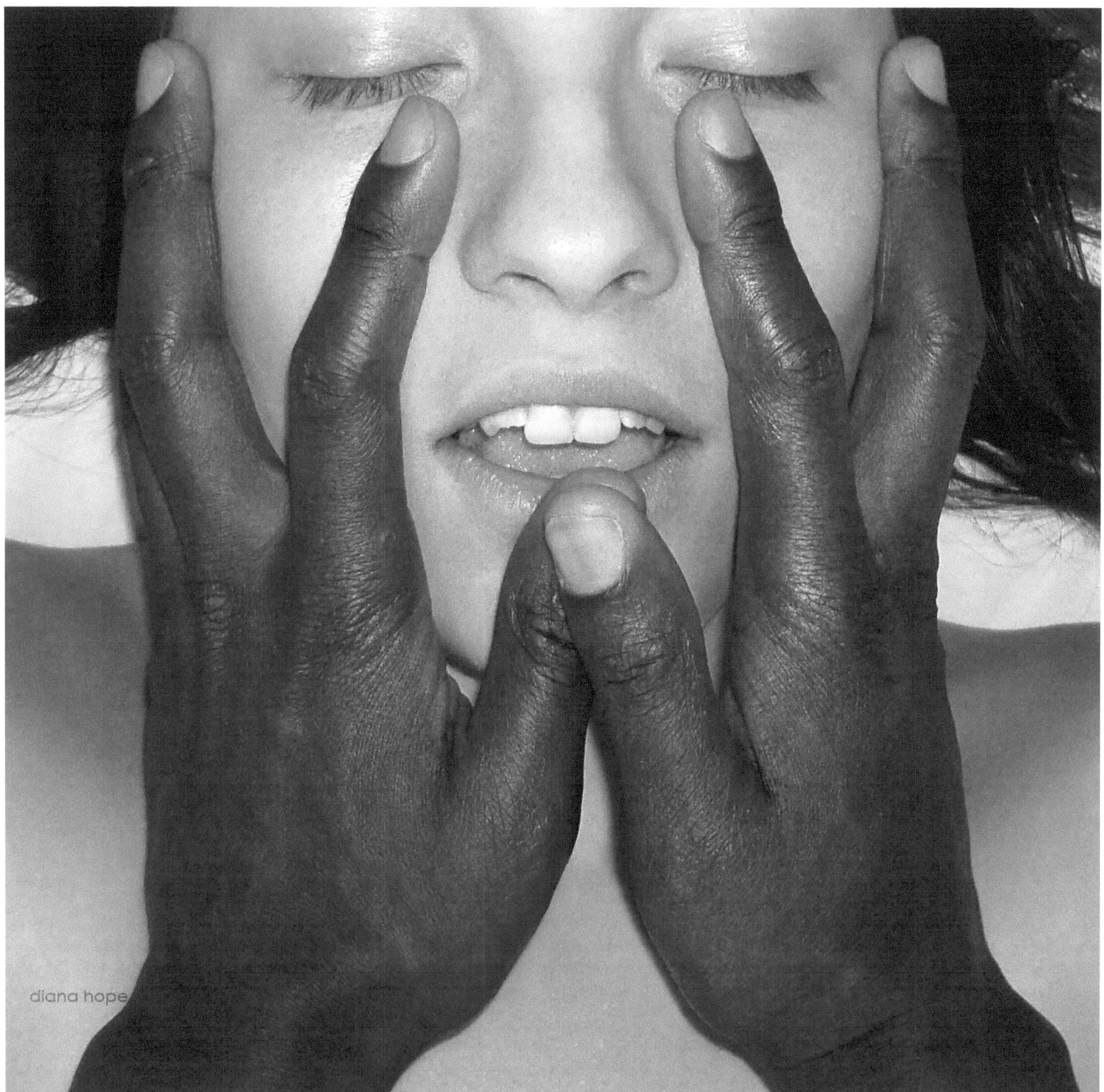
diana hope

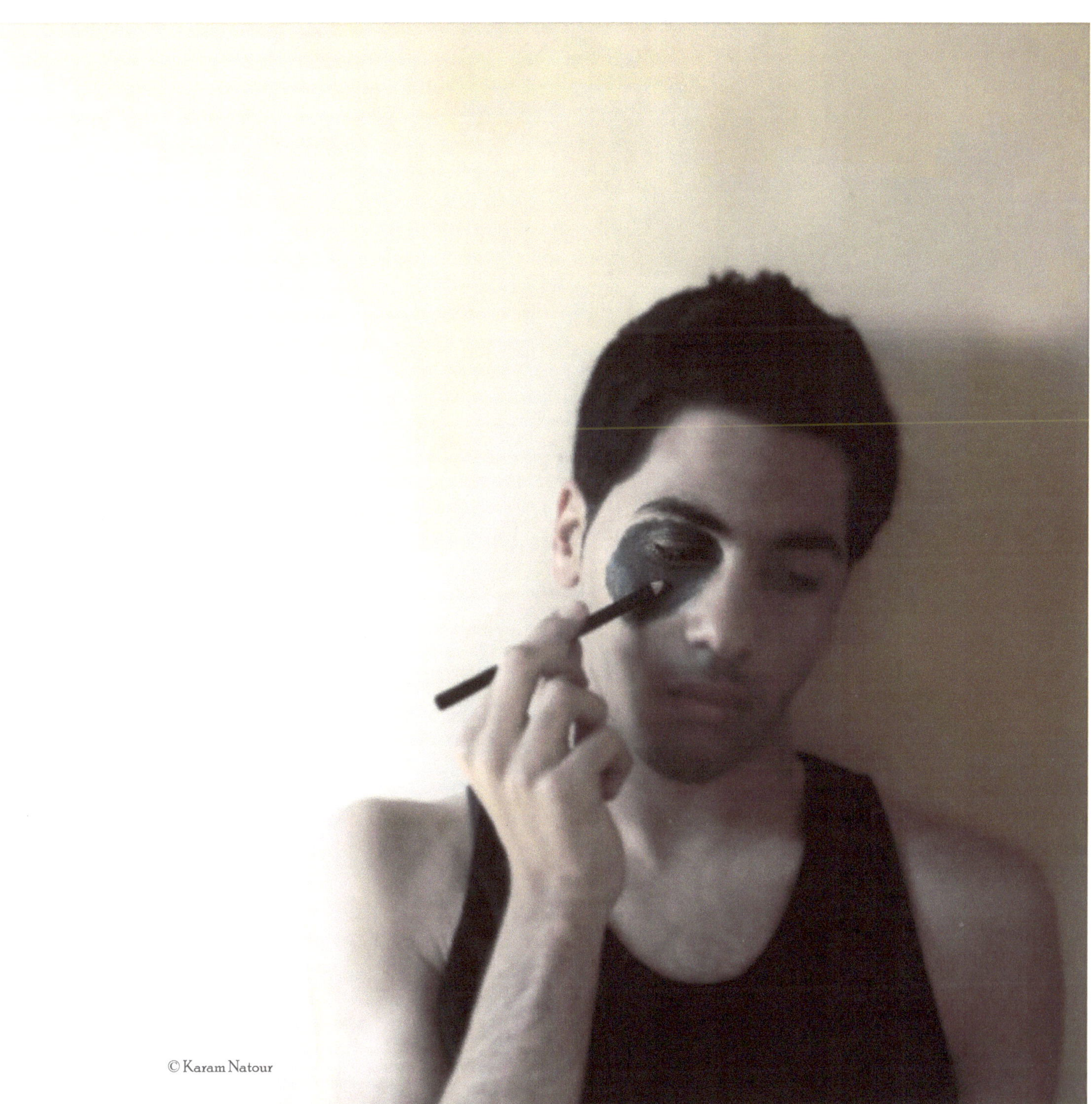
© Karam Natour

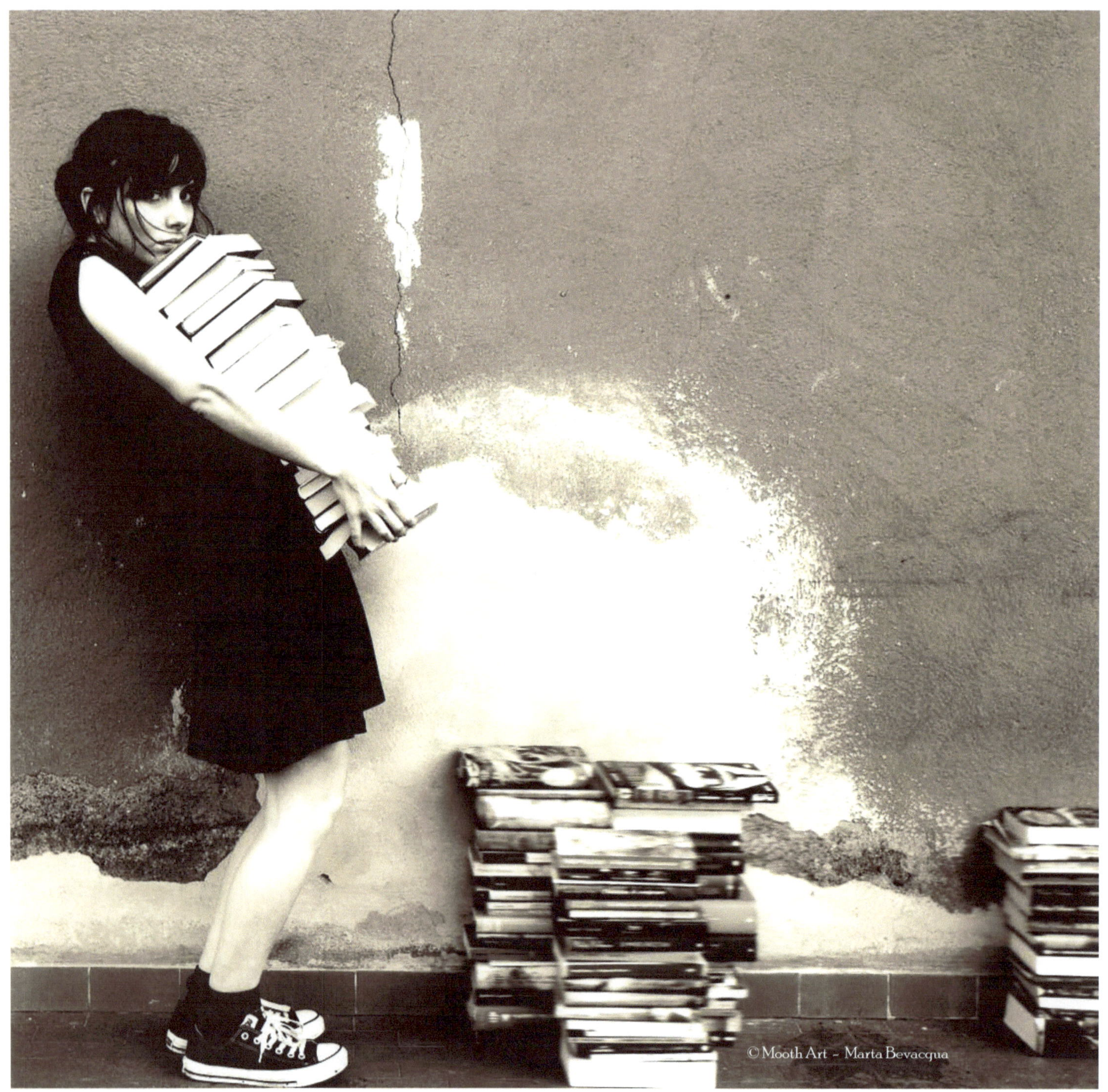
© Mooth Art - Marta Bevacqua

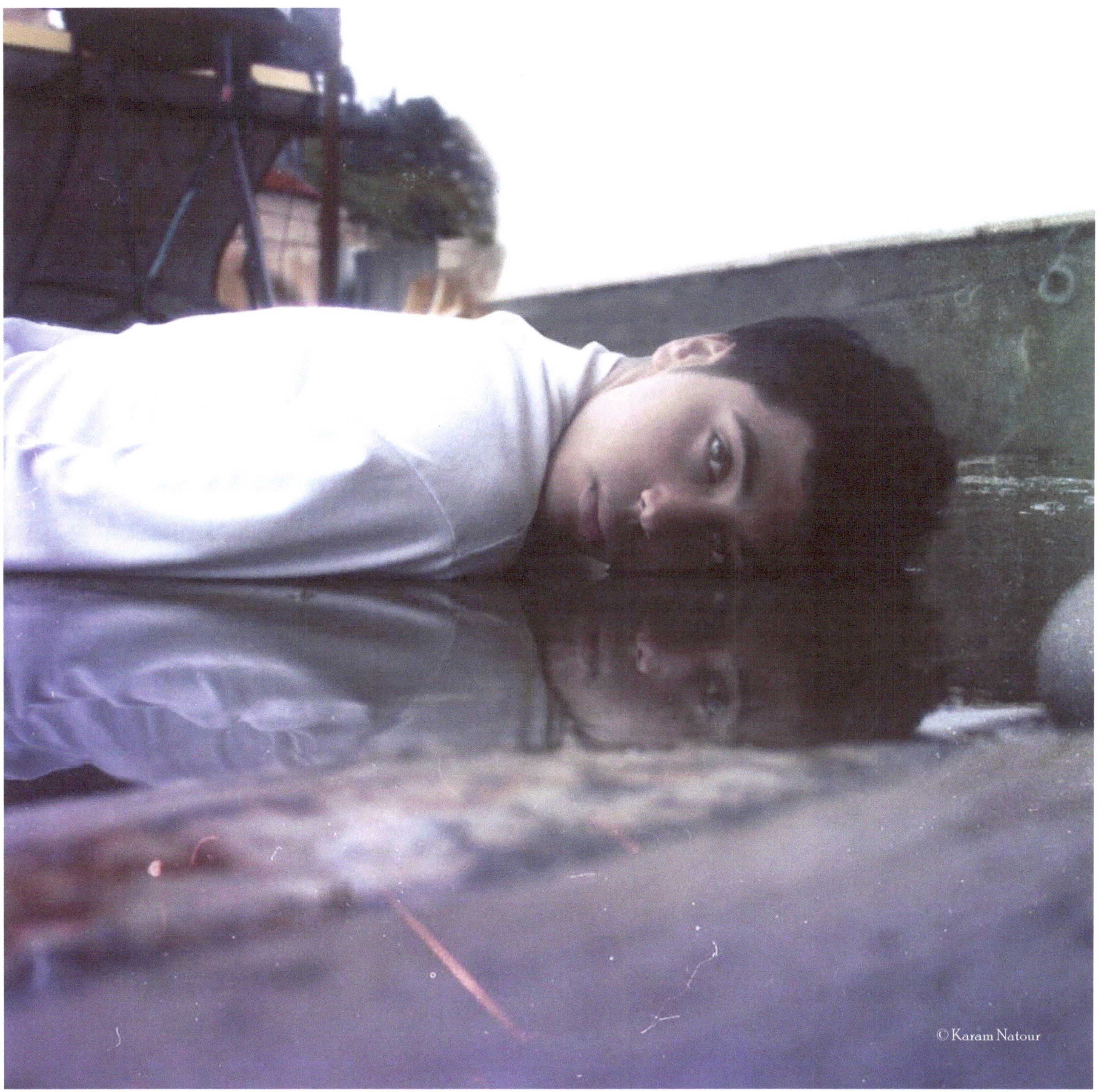
© Karam Natour

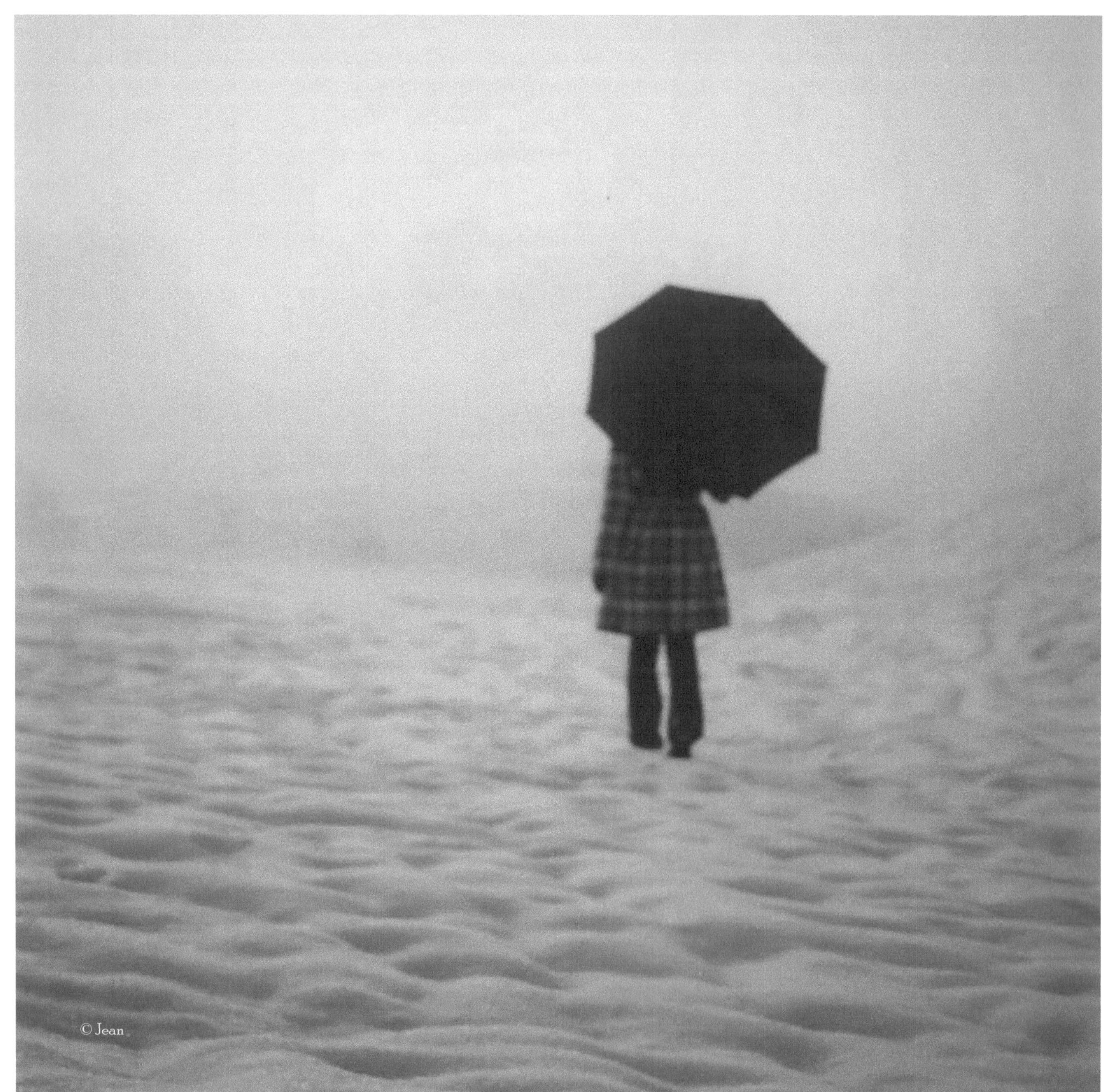
© Jean

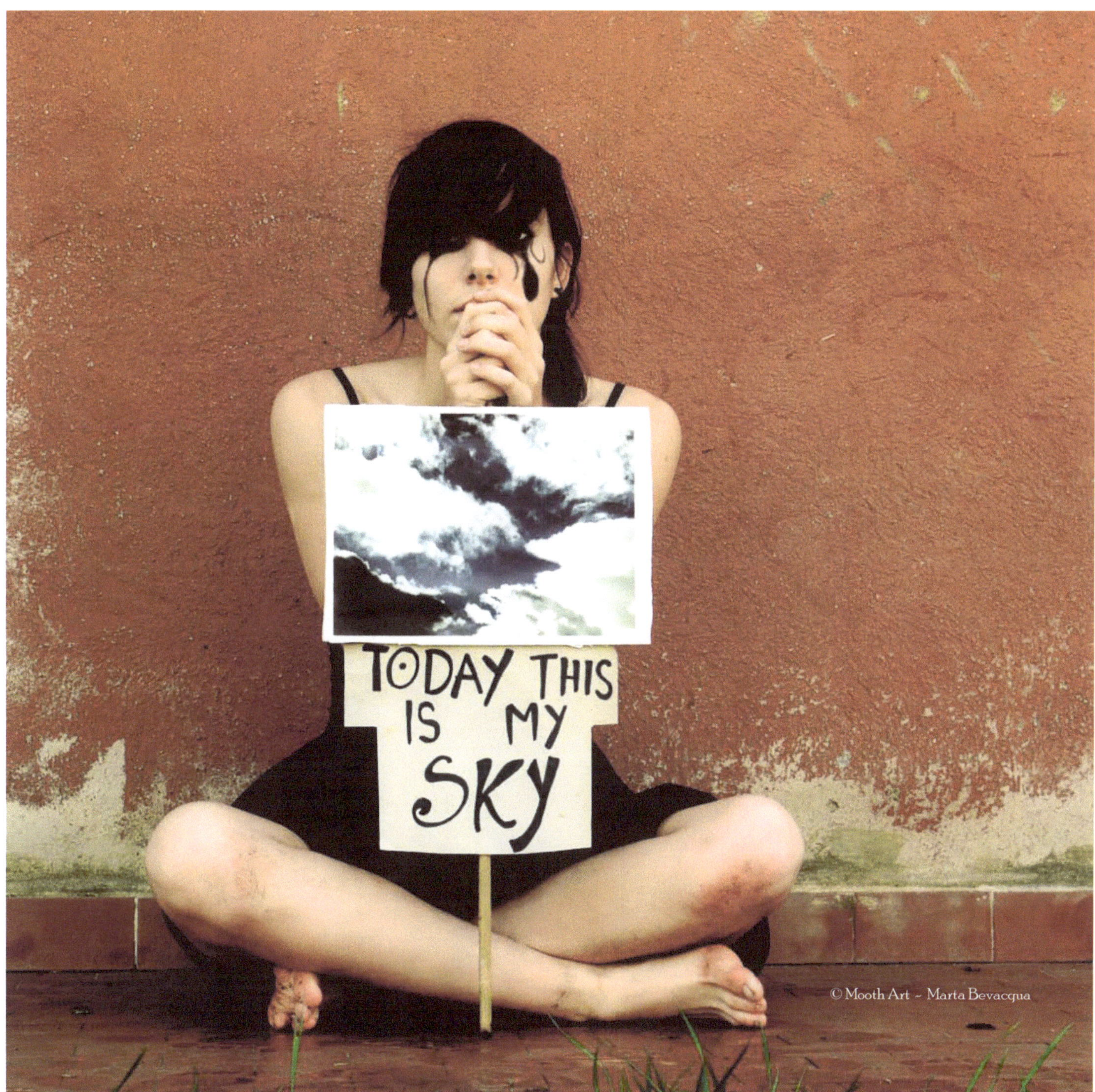
TODAY THIS
IS MY
SKY
© Mooth Art - Marta Bevacqua

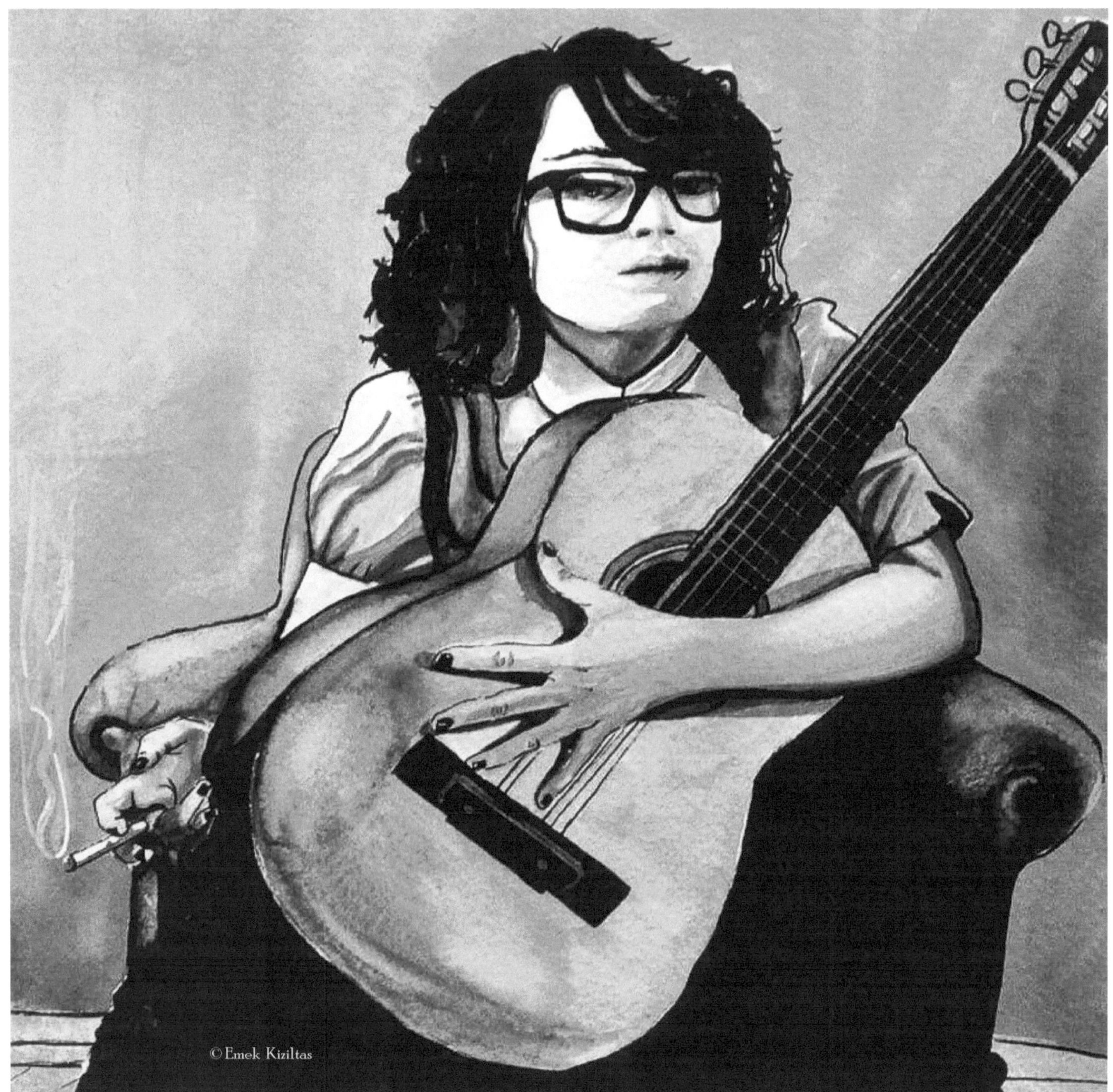
©Emek Kiziltas

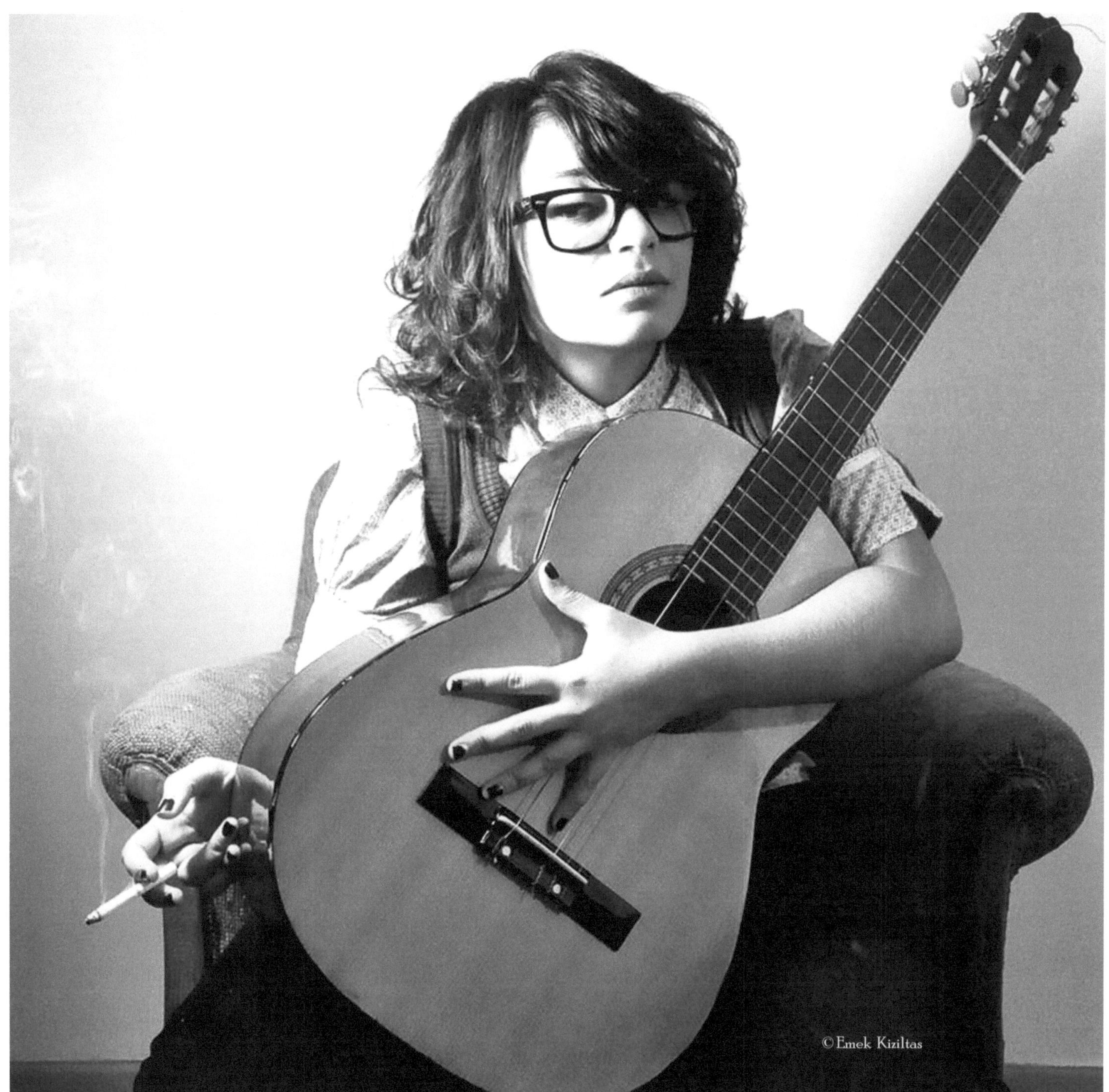
©Emek Kiziltas

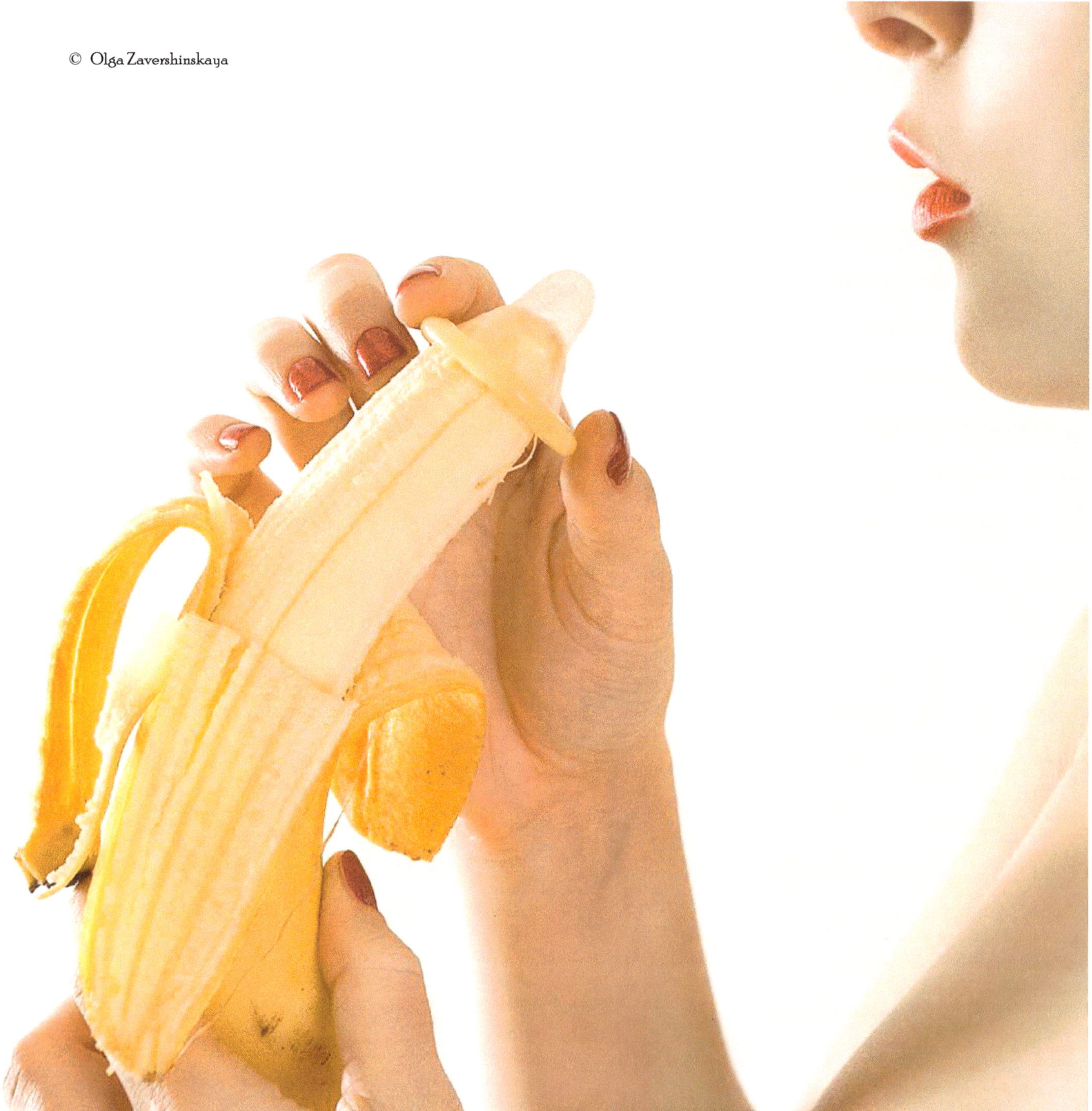

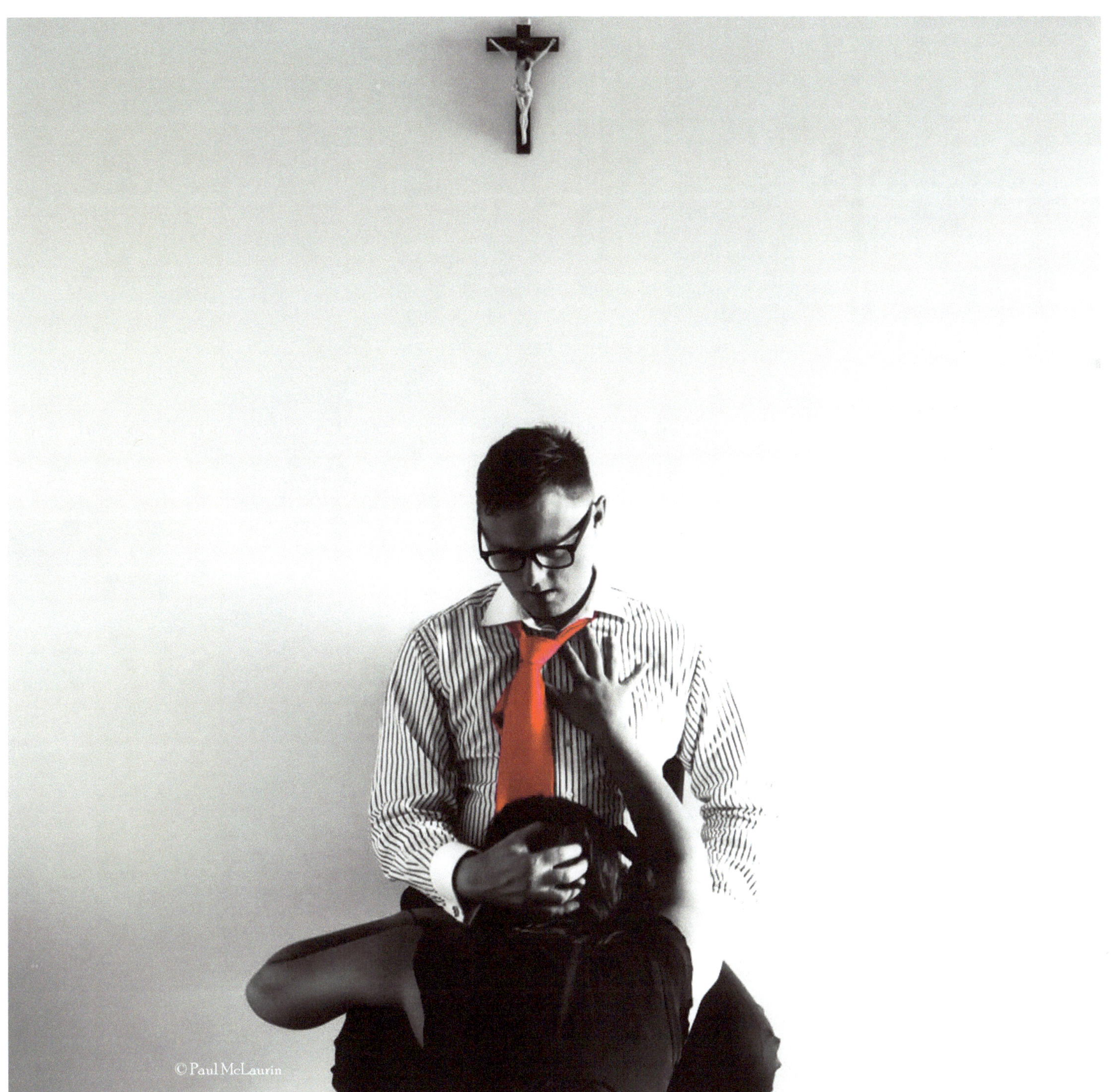
© Paul McLaurin

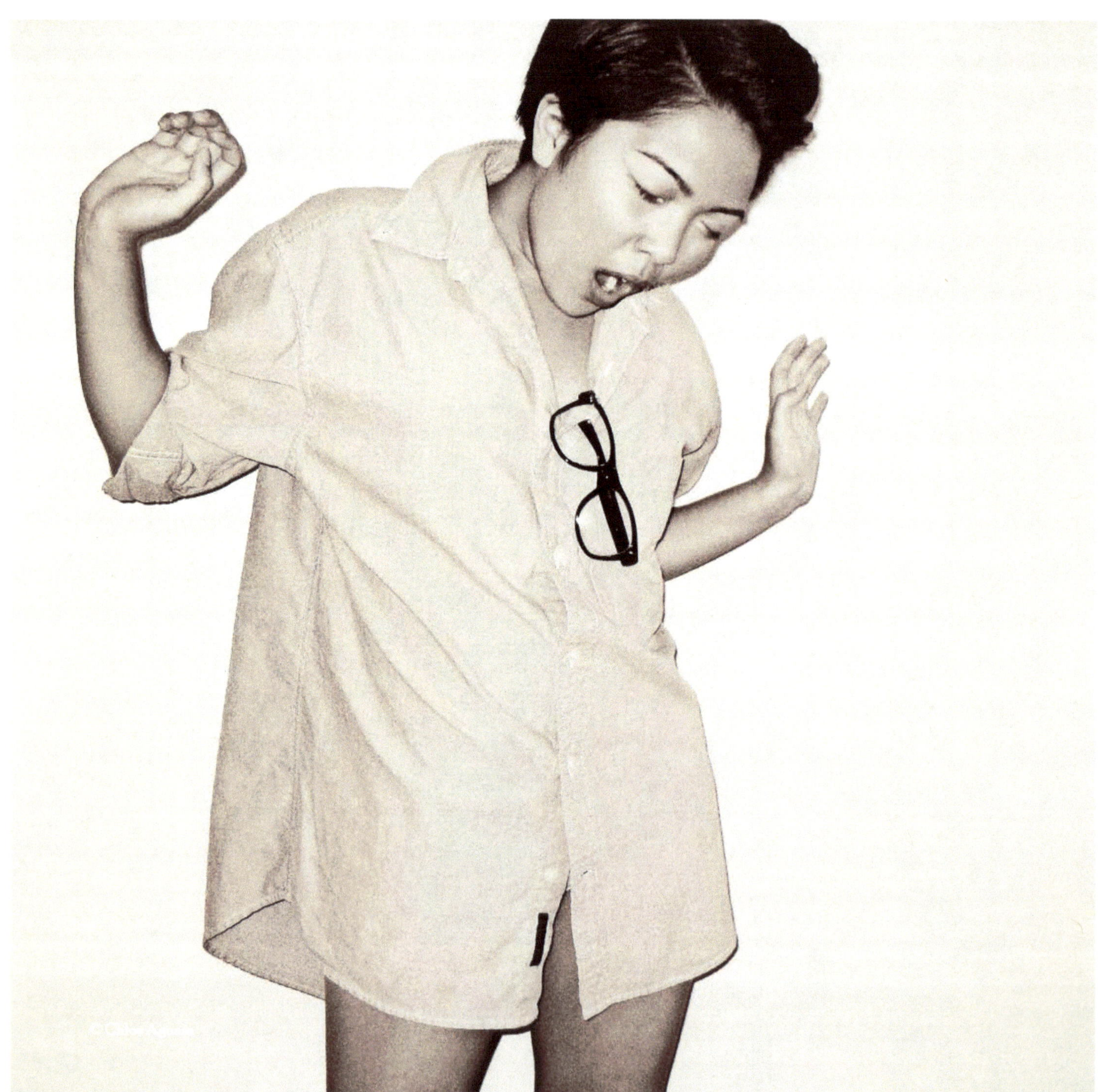

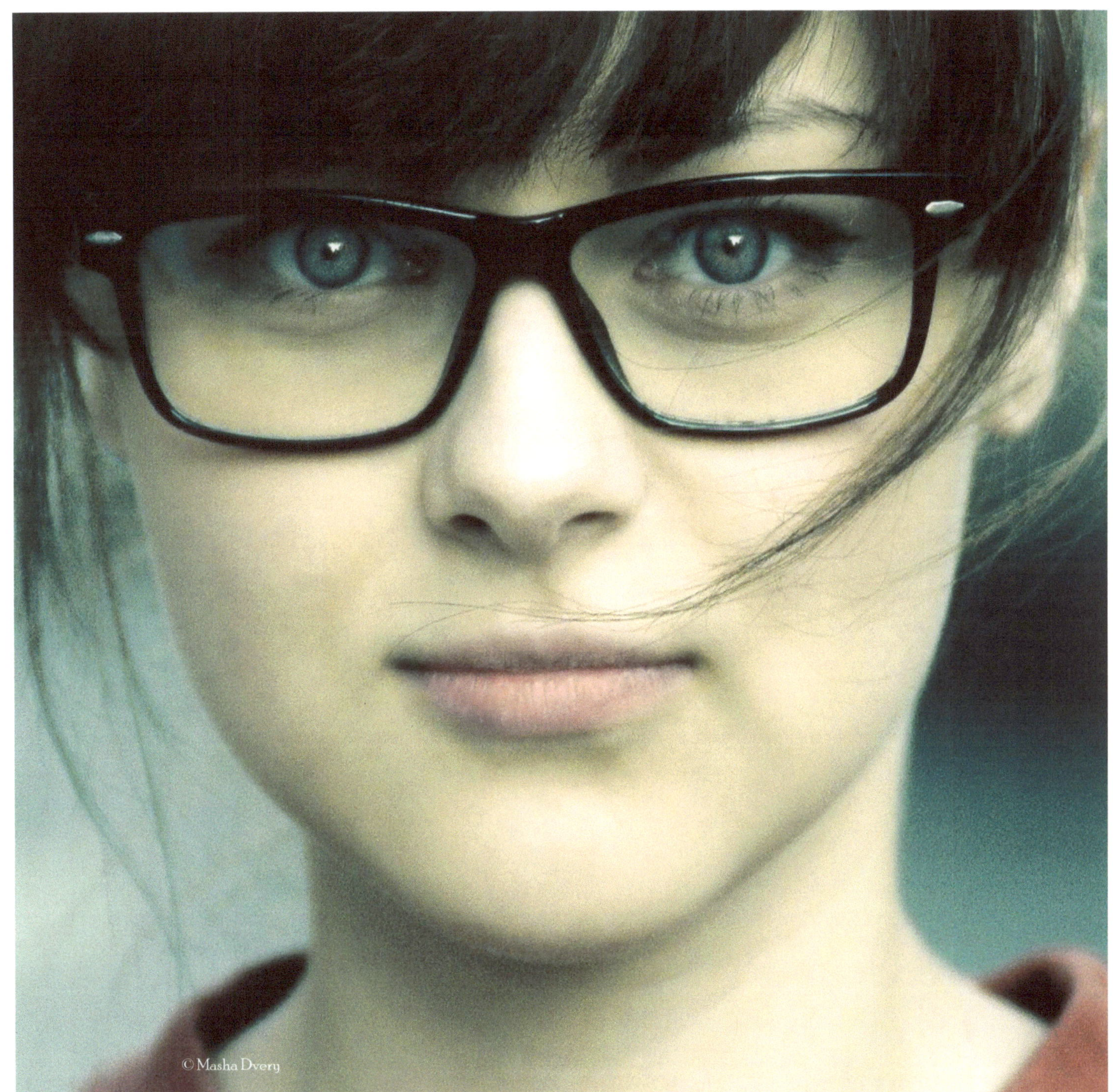
© Masha Dvery

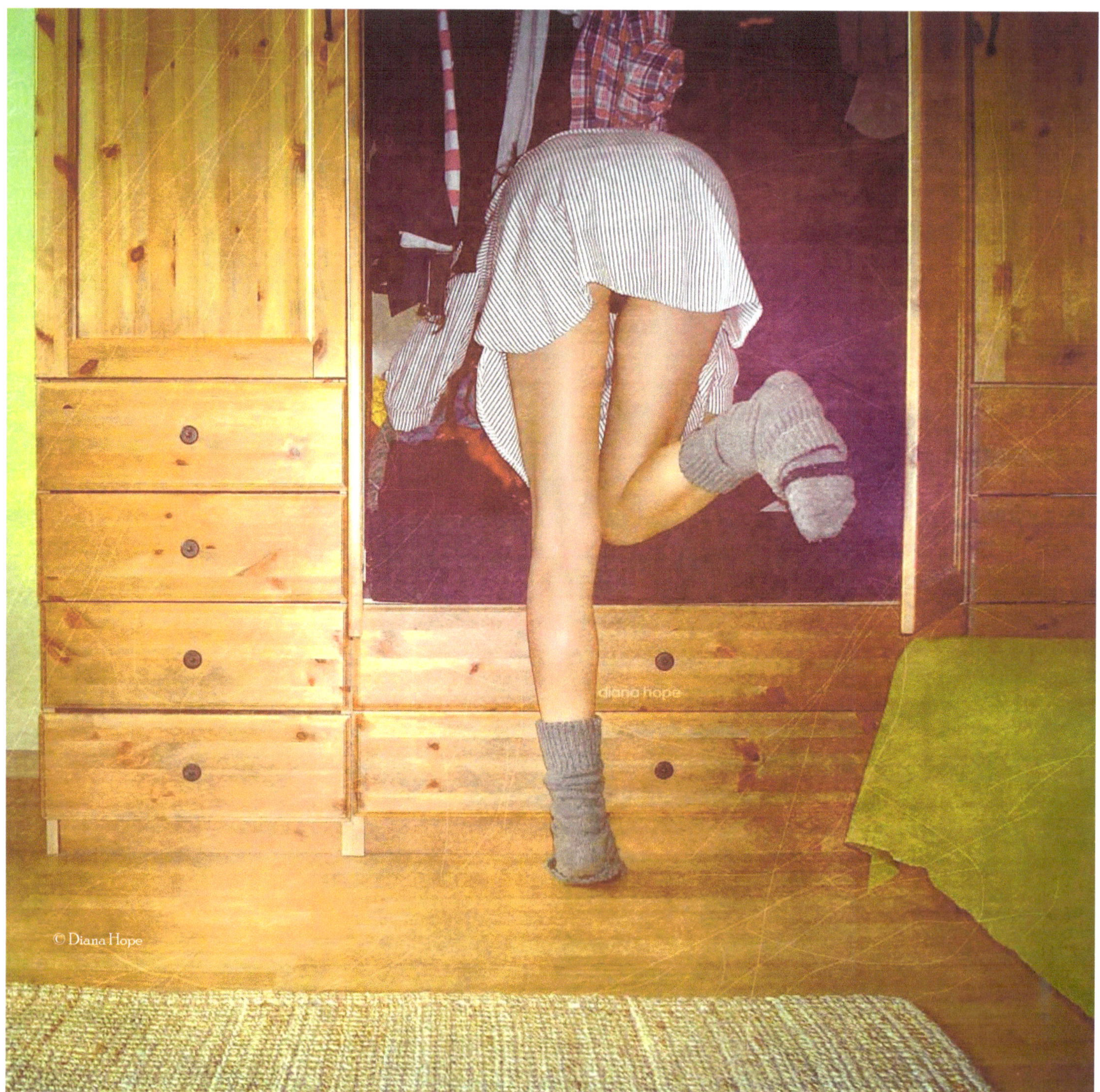
diana hope
© Diana Hope

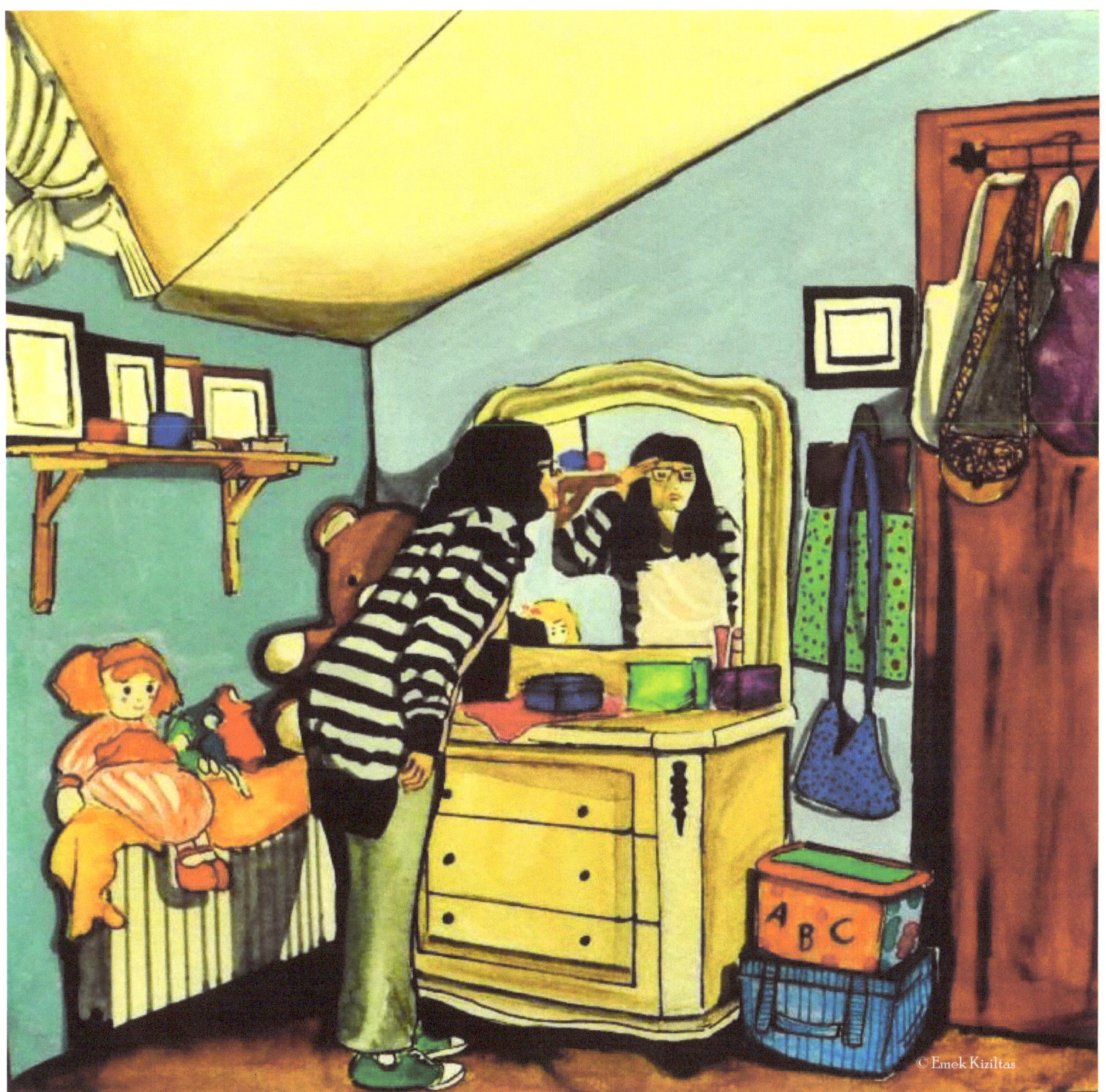
A B C
© Emek Kiziltas

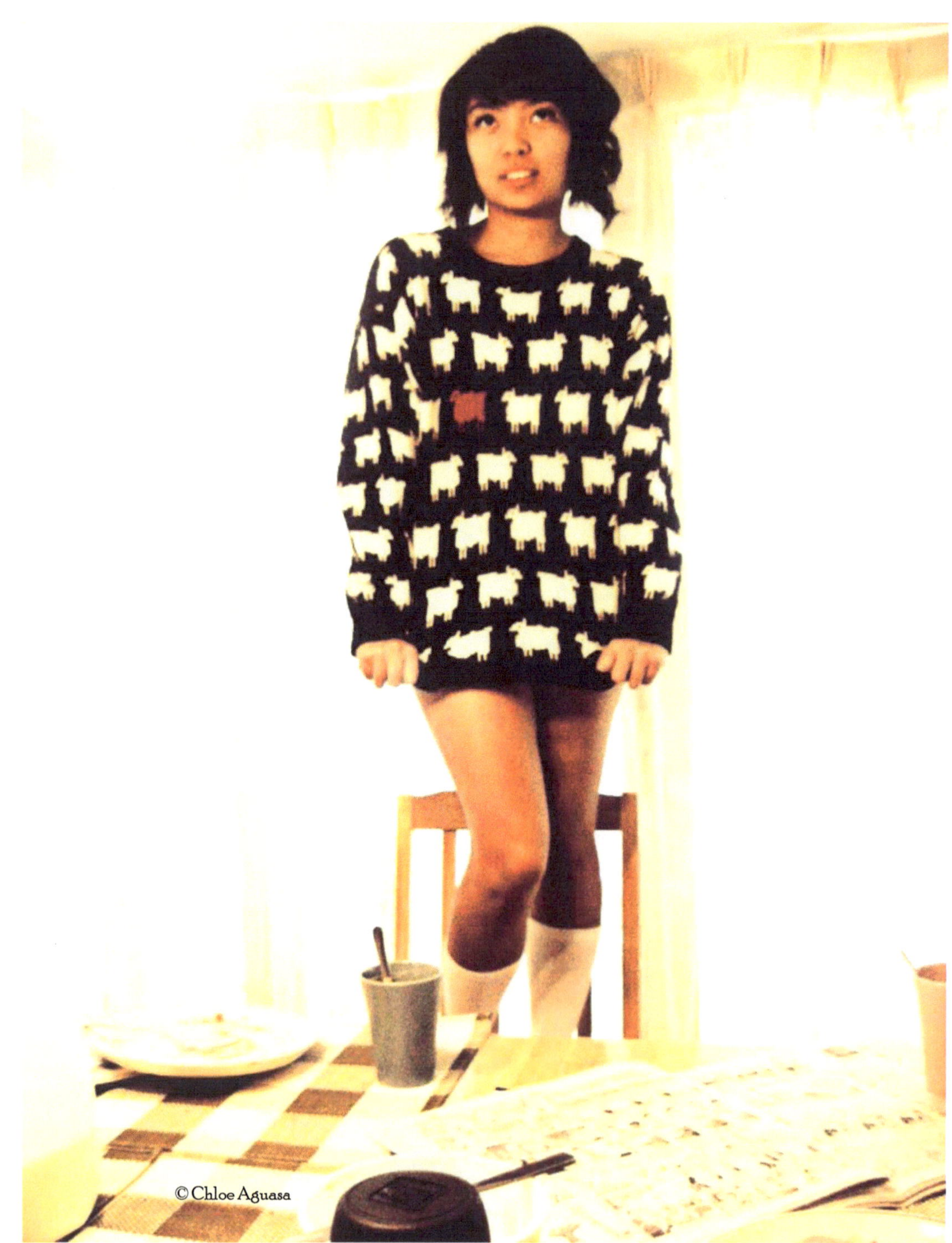
© Chloe Aguasa

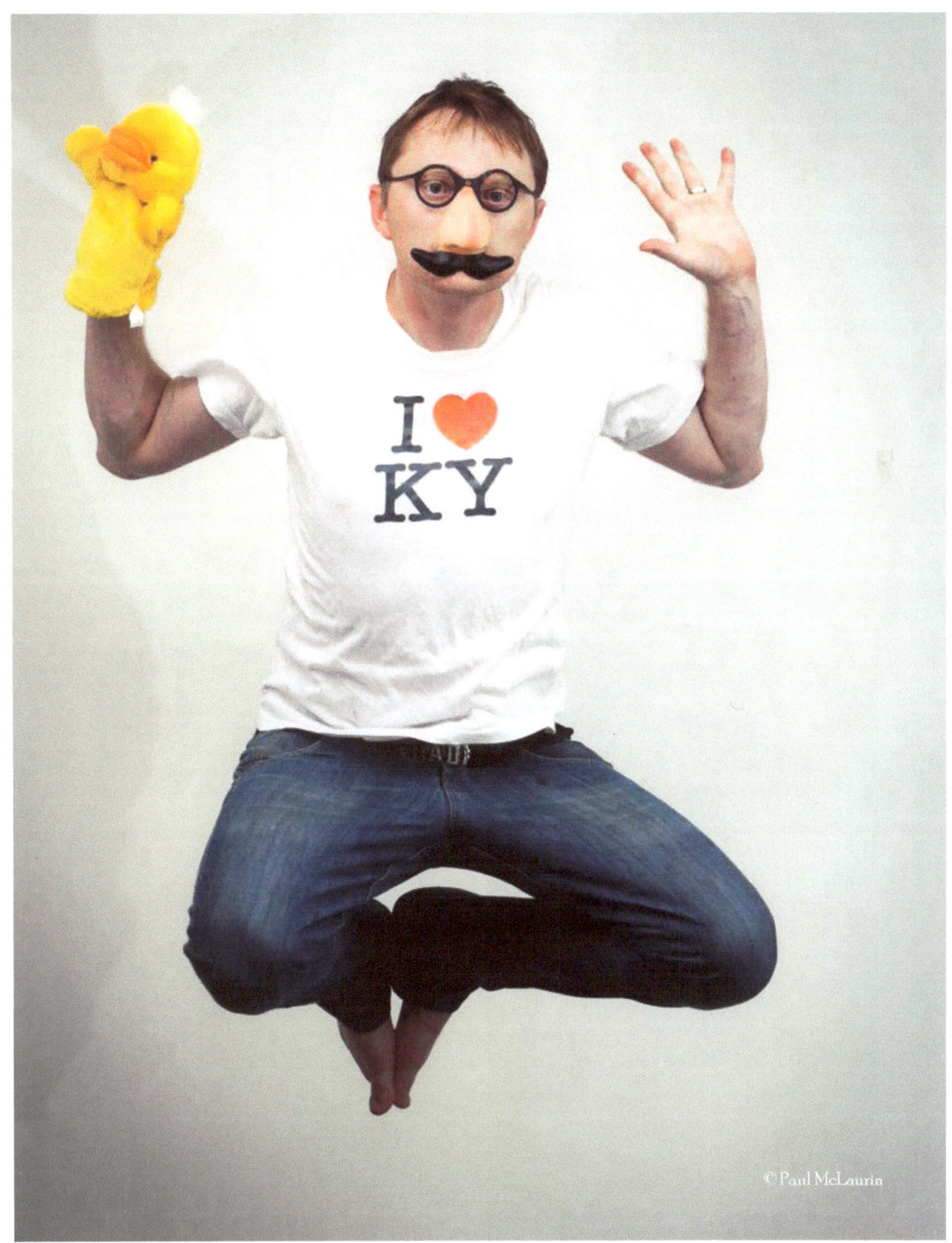
I ♥
KY
© Paul McLaurin

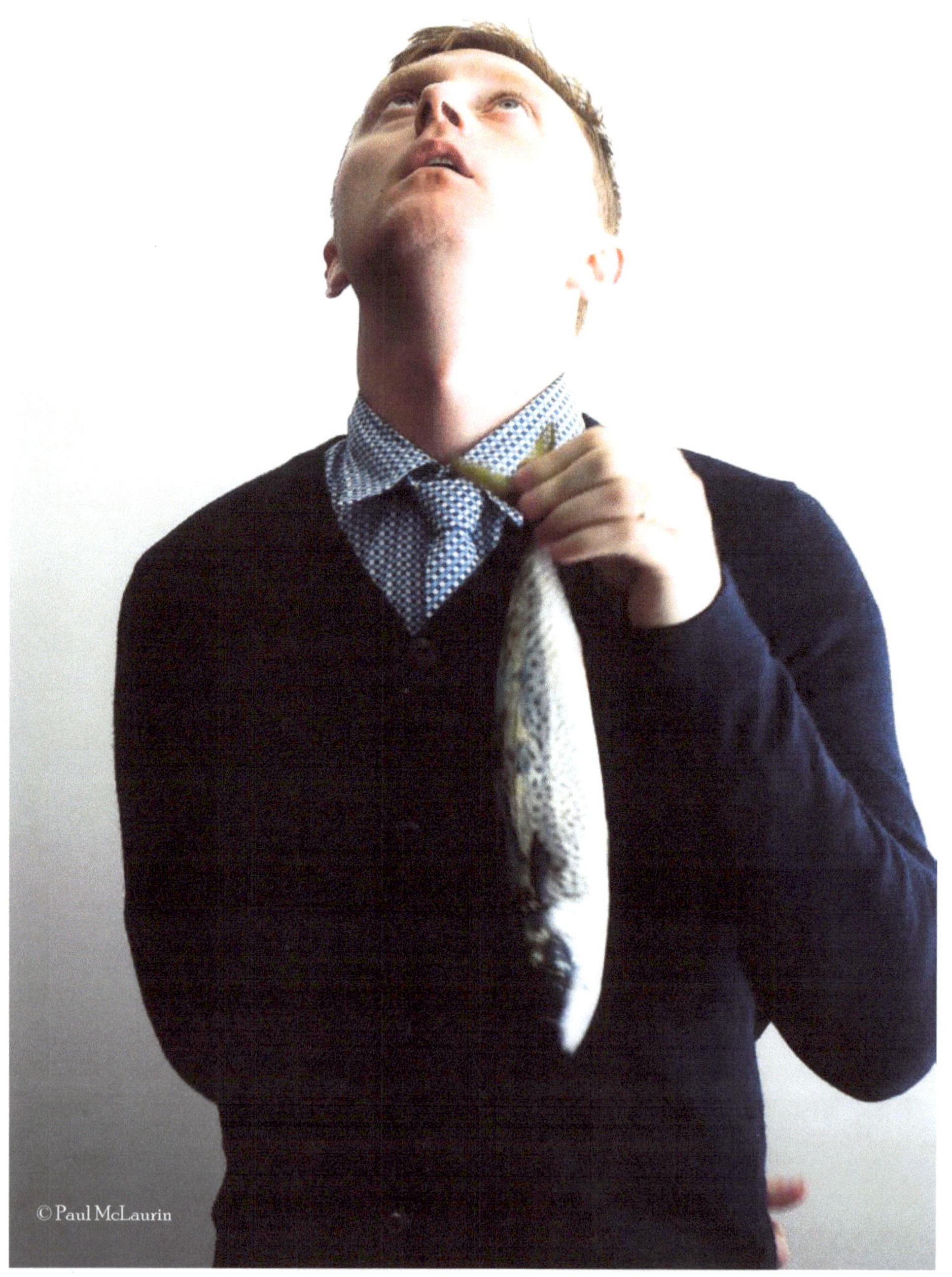
© Paul McLaurin

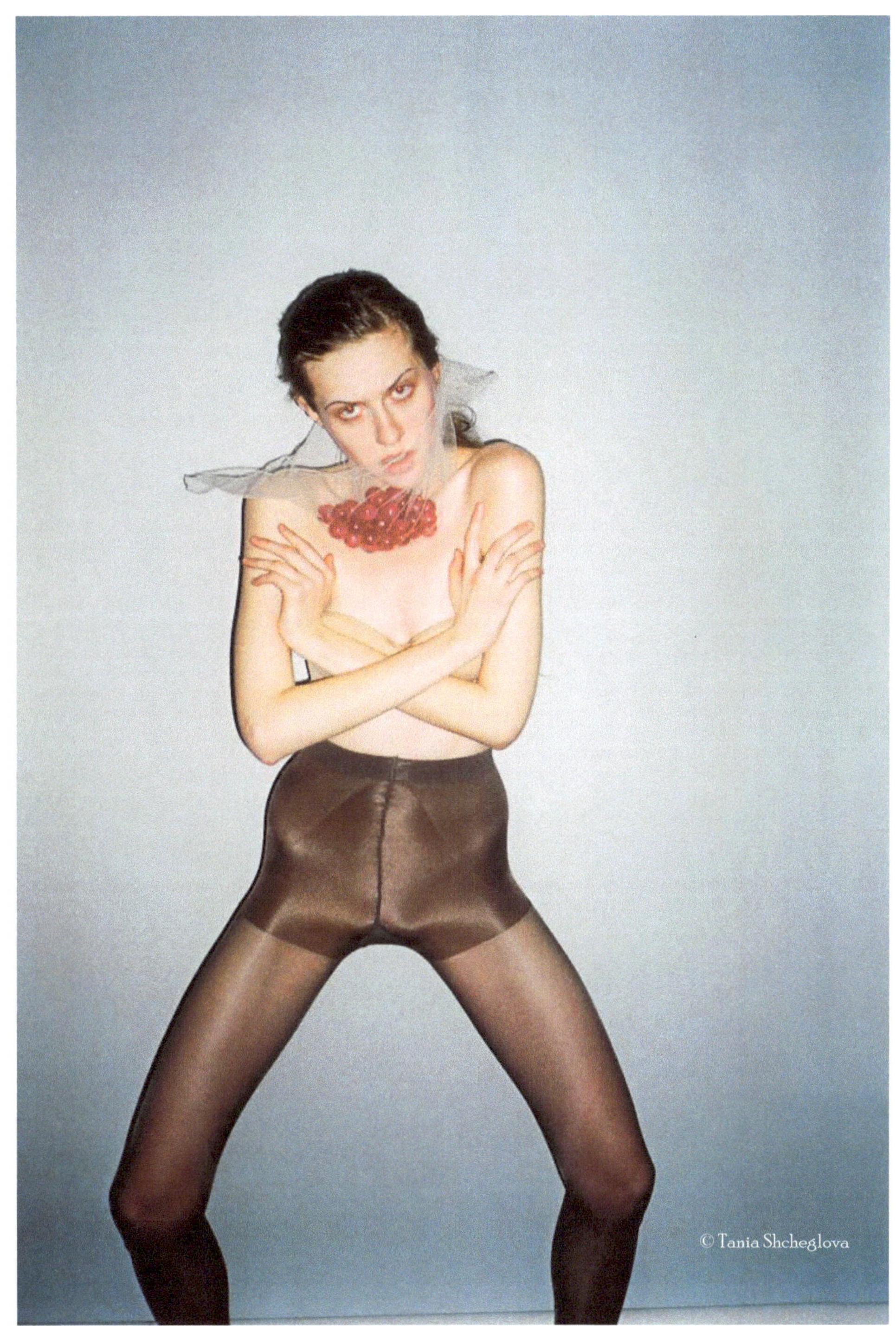

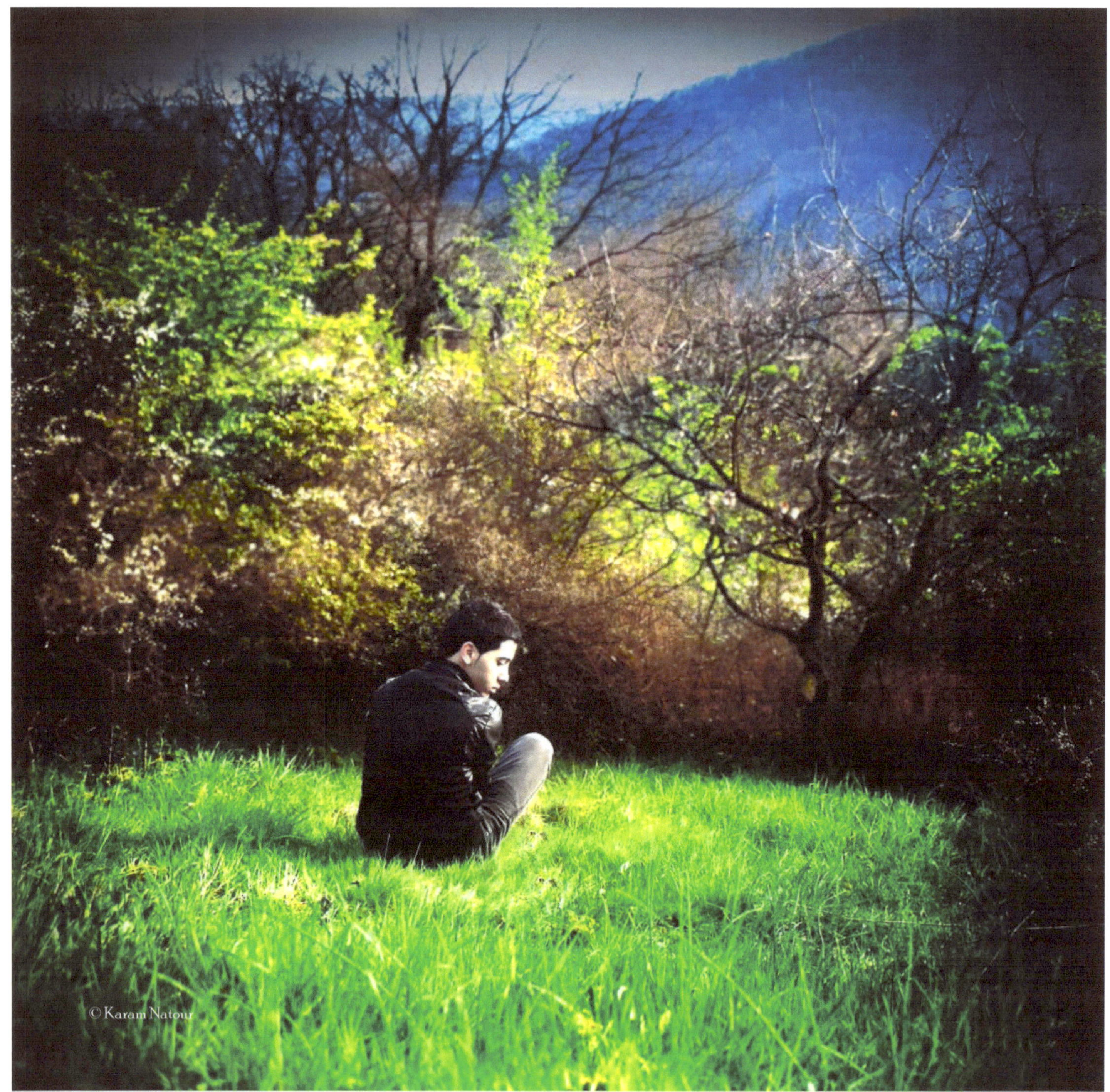
© Karam Natour

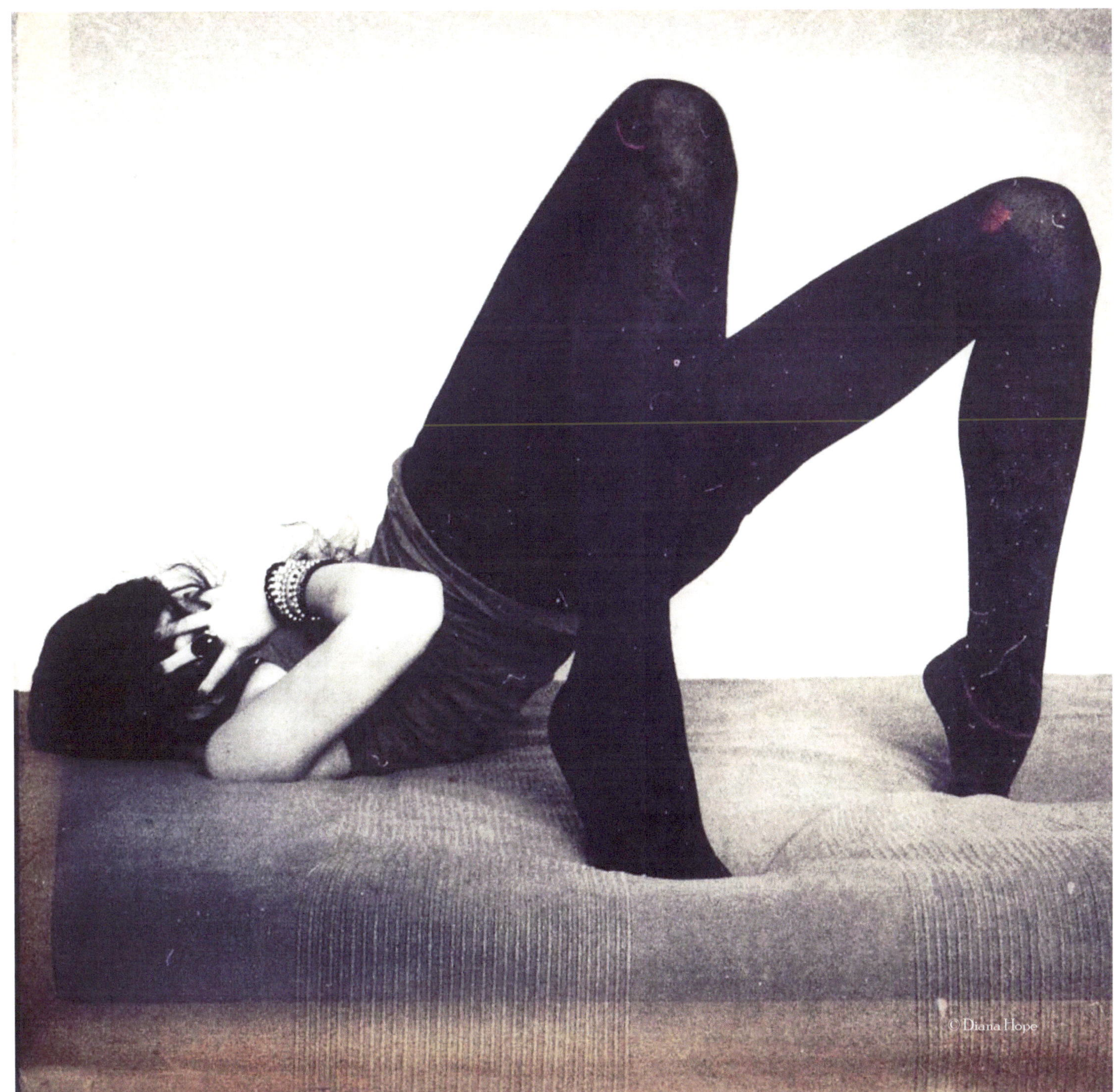
© Diana Hope

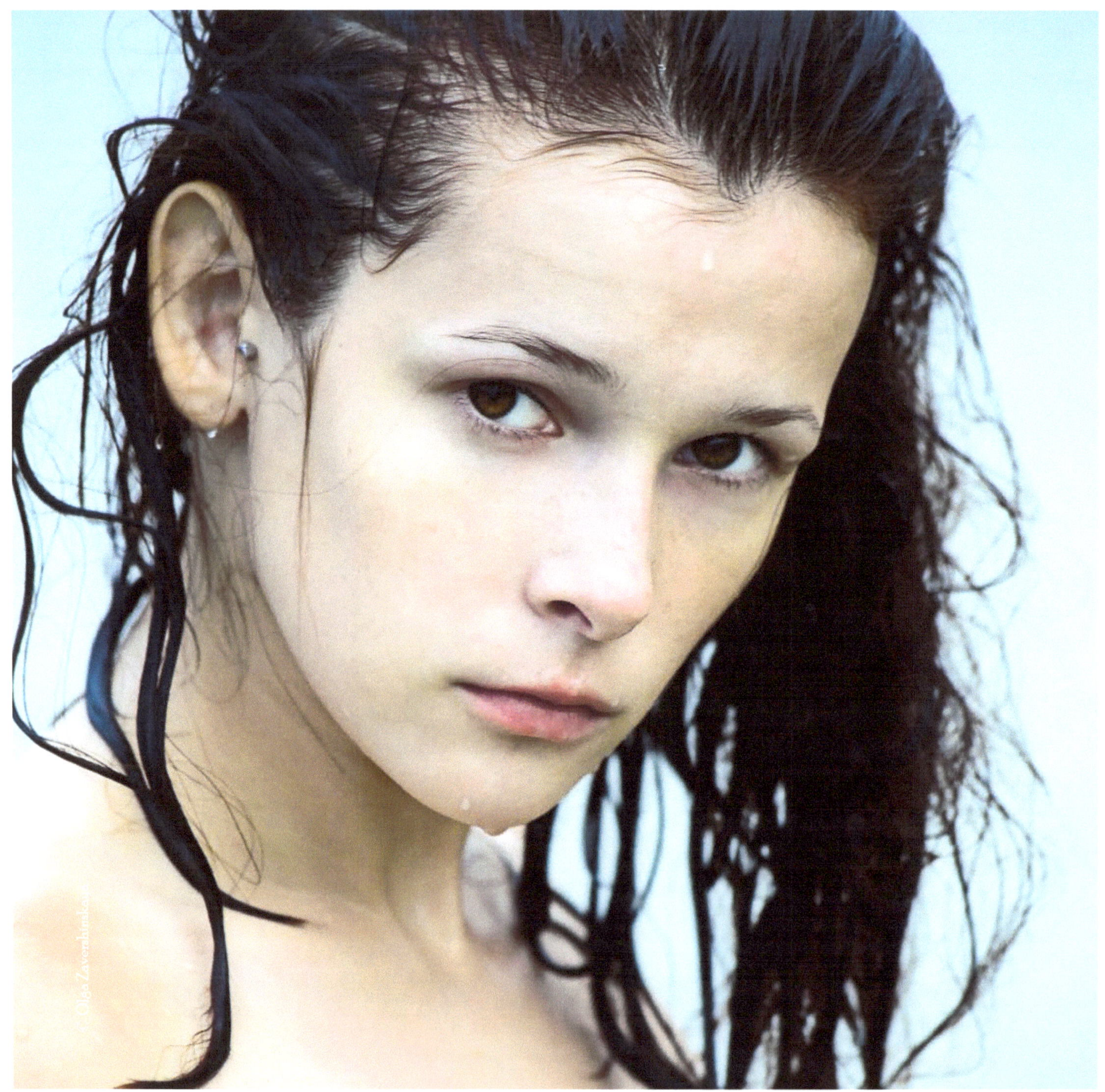
© Olga Zavershinska

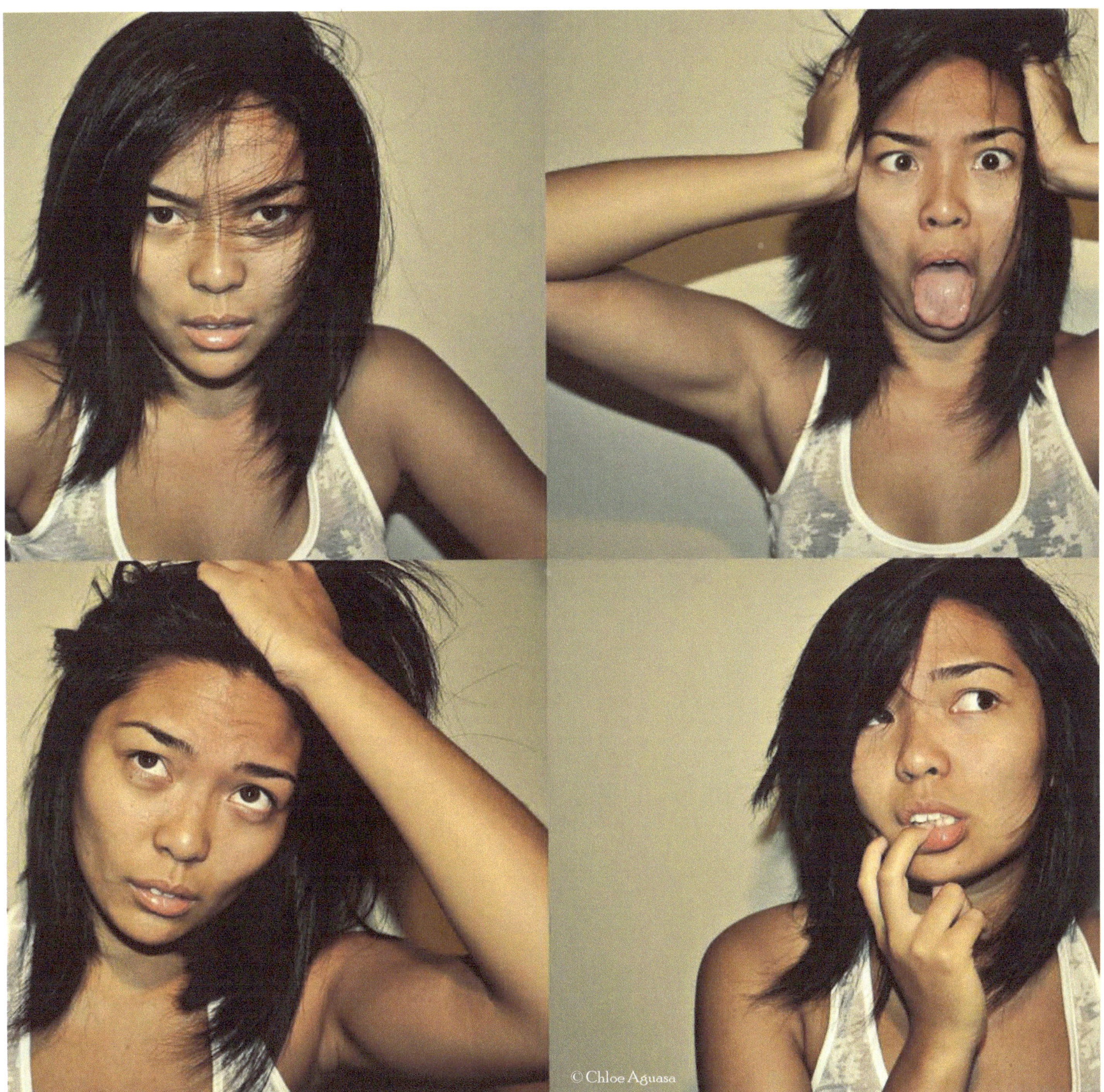
© Chloe Aguasa

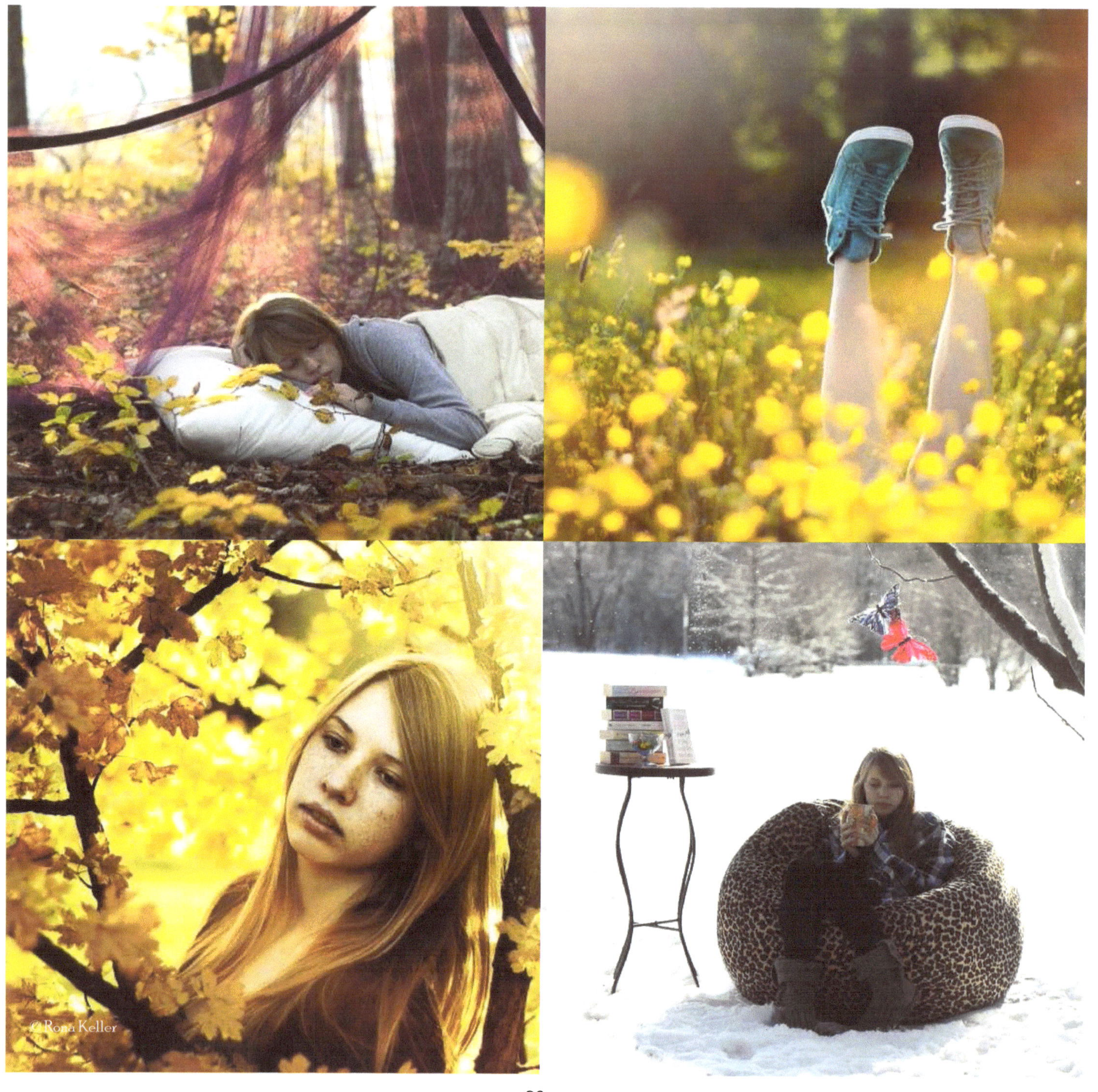
© Rona Keller

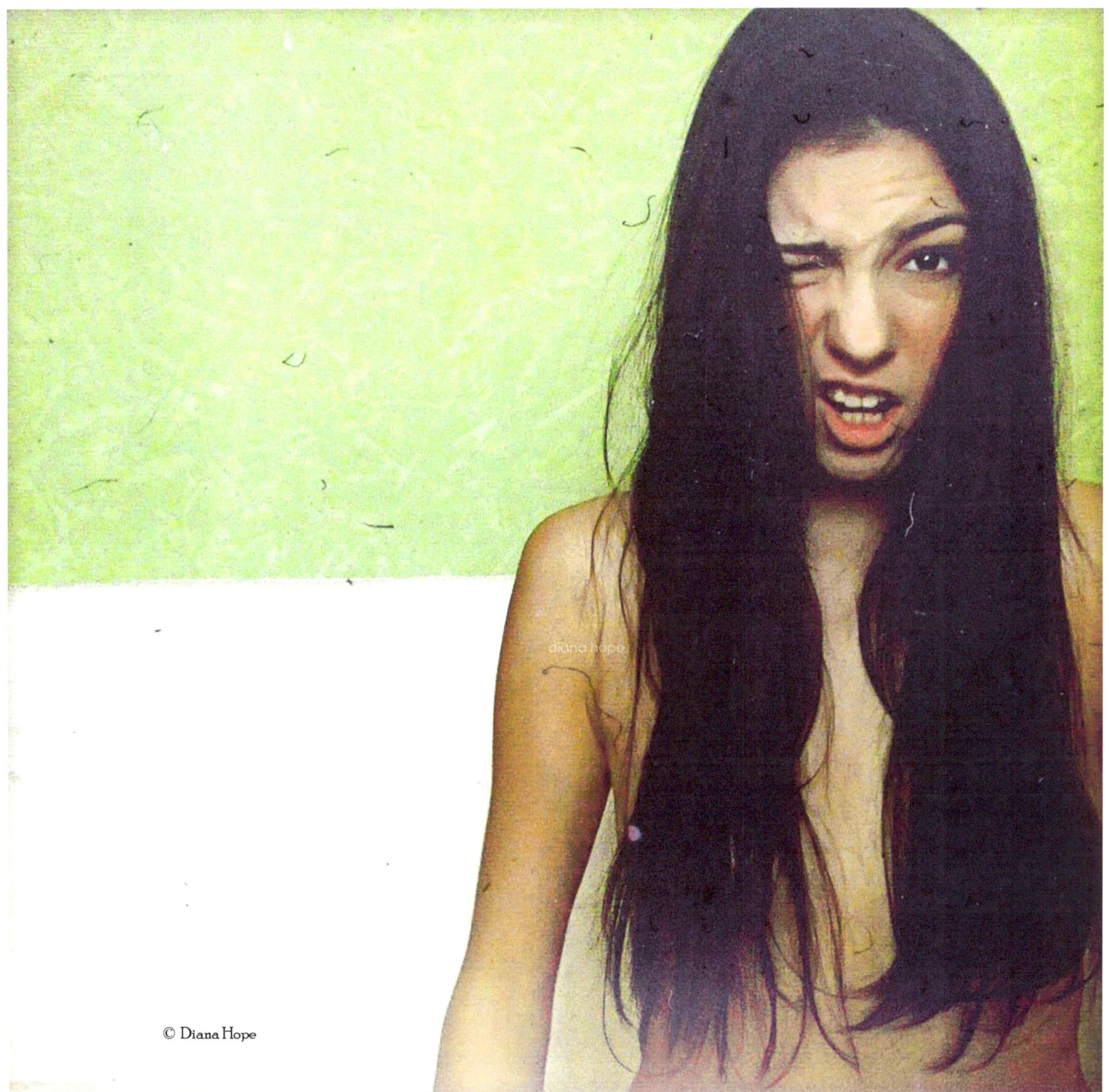
diana hope

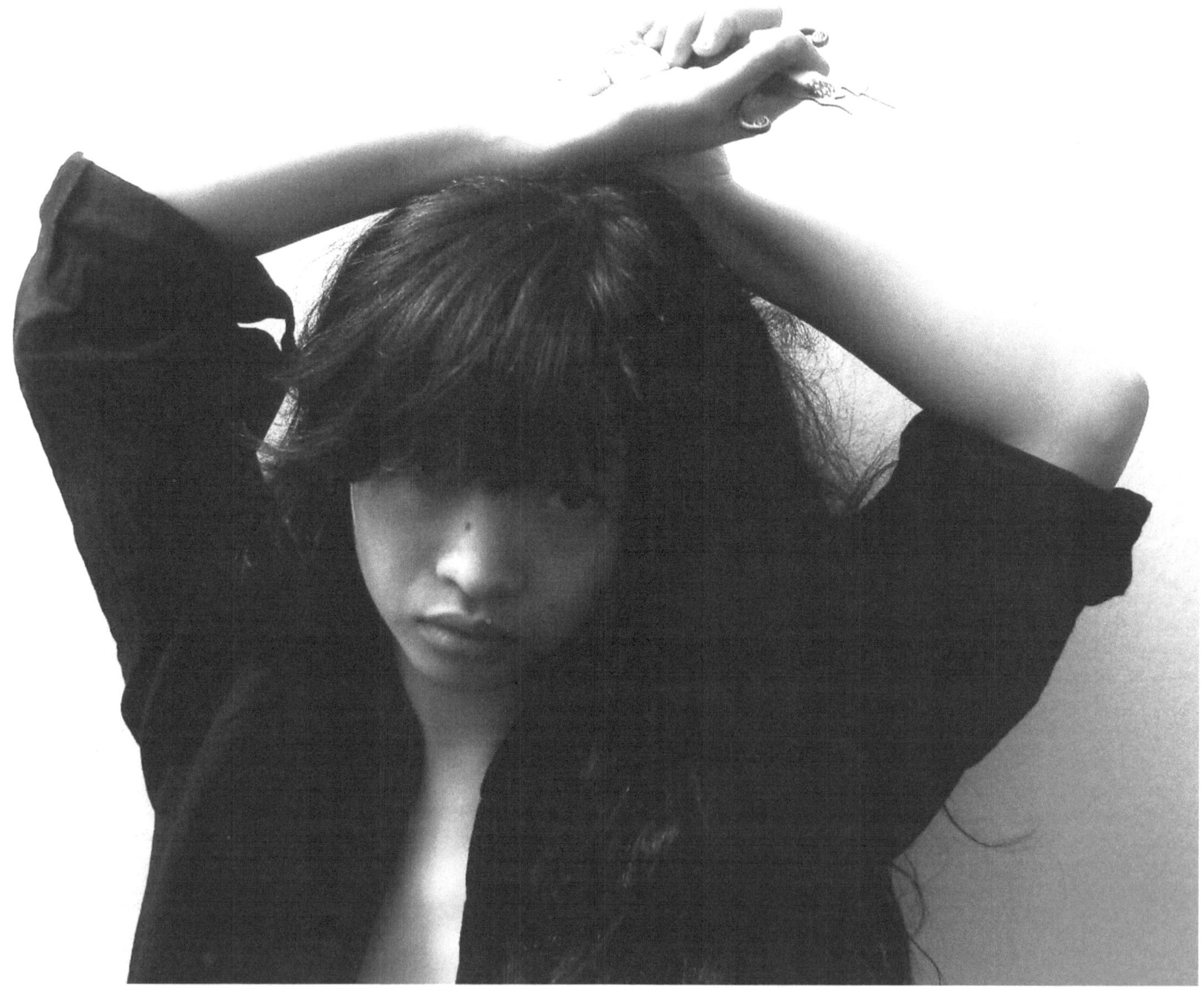

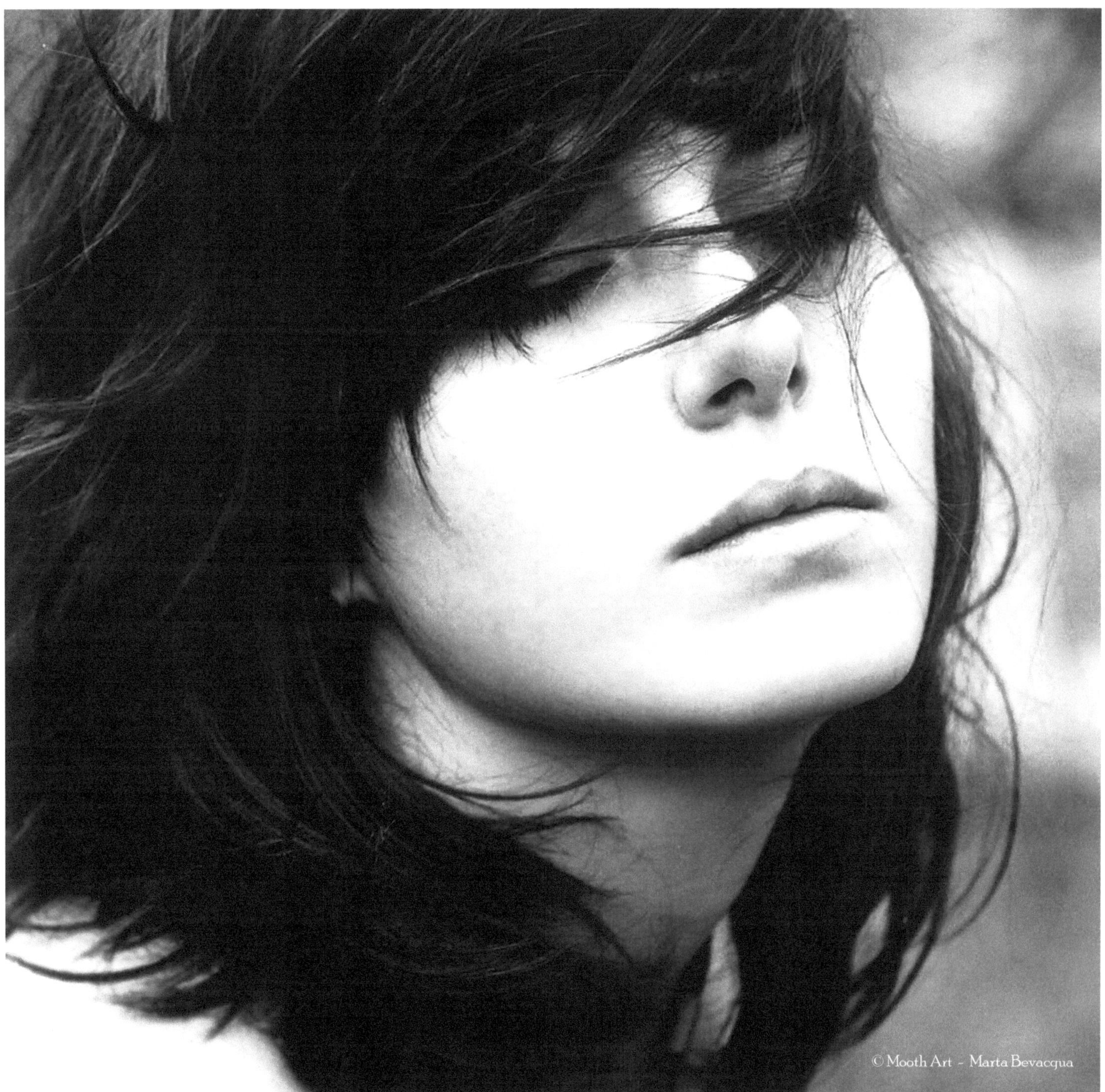
© Mooth Art - Marta Bevacqua

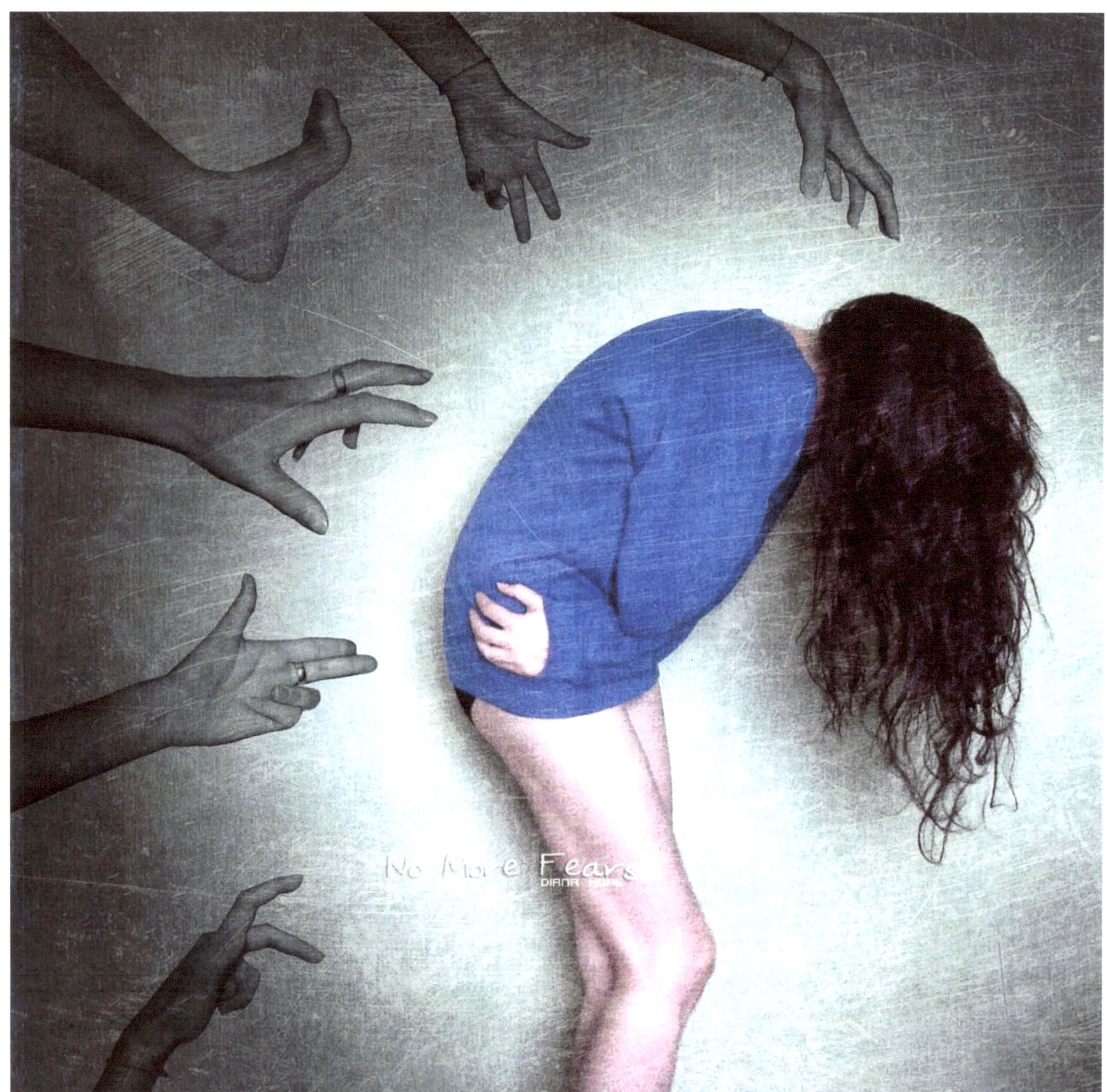
No More Fears
DIANA

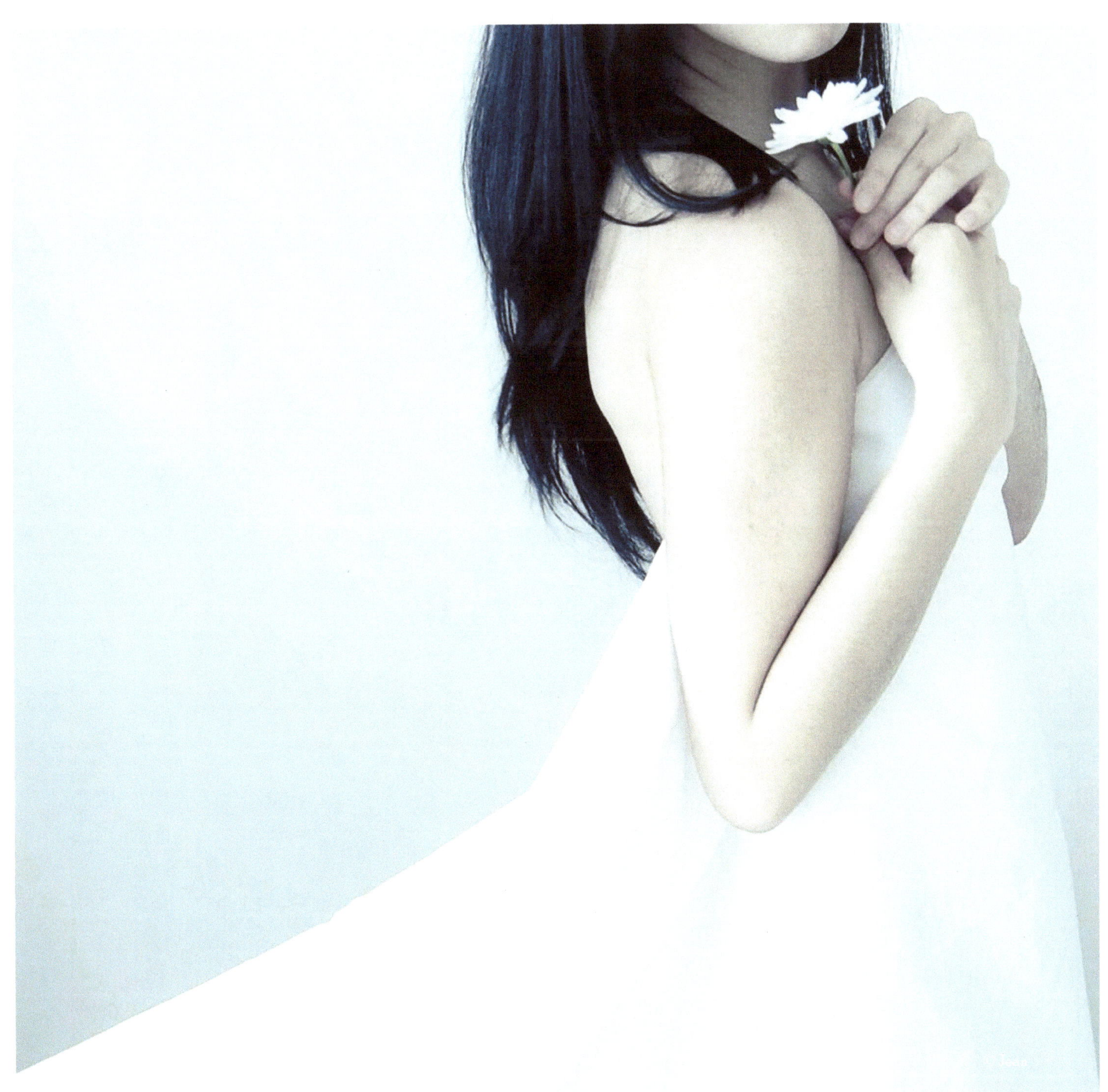

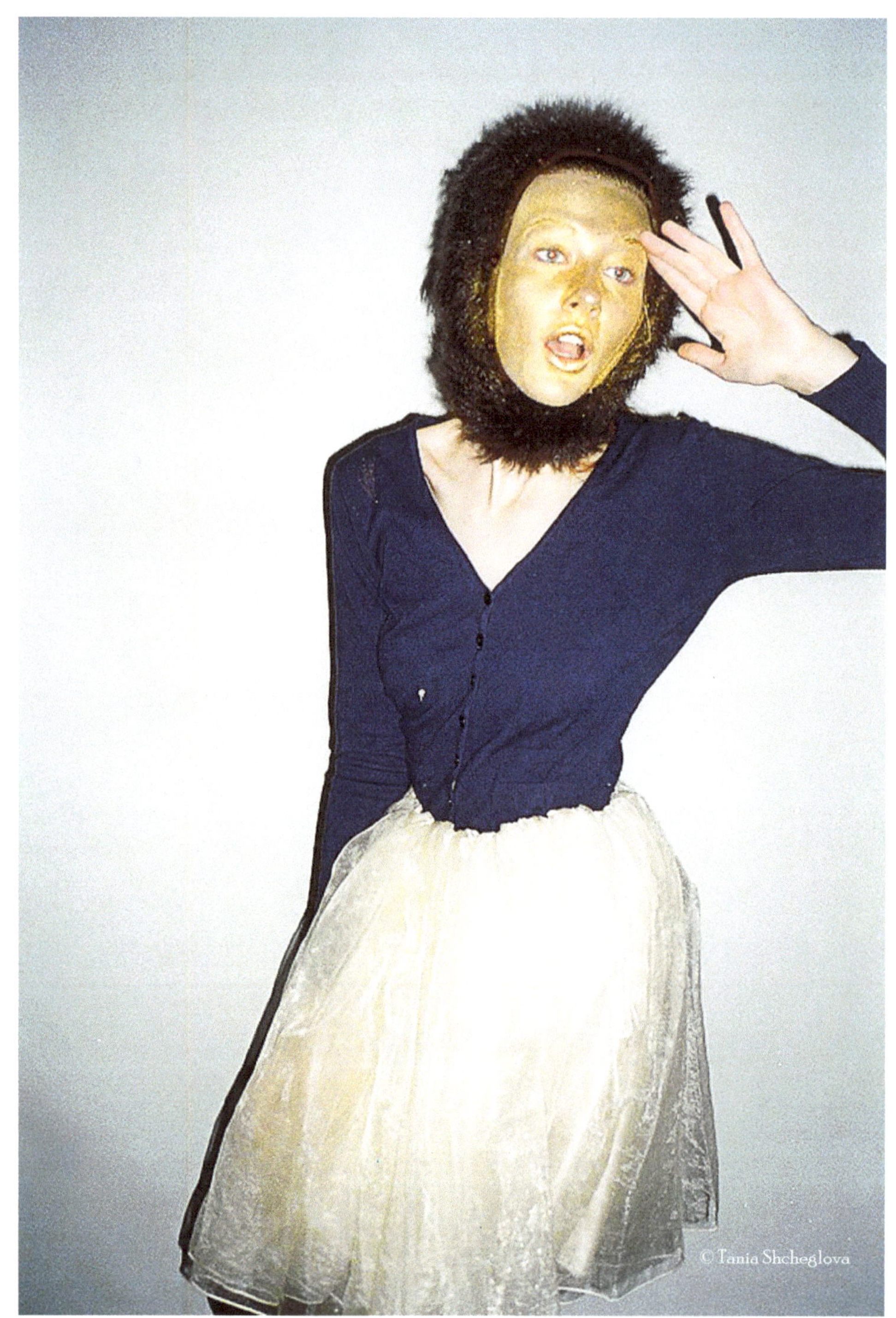

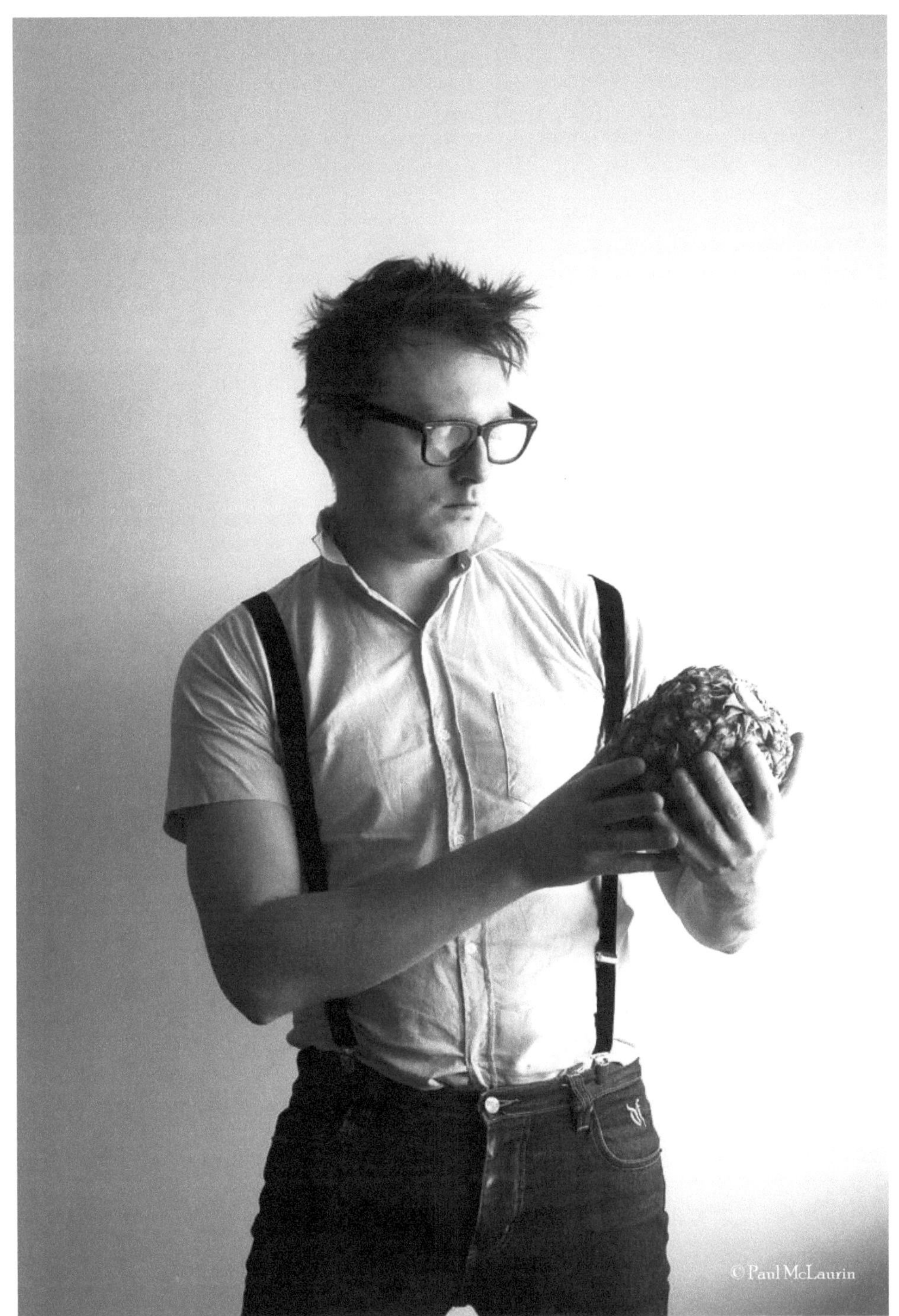
© Paul McLaurin

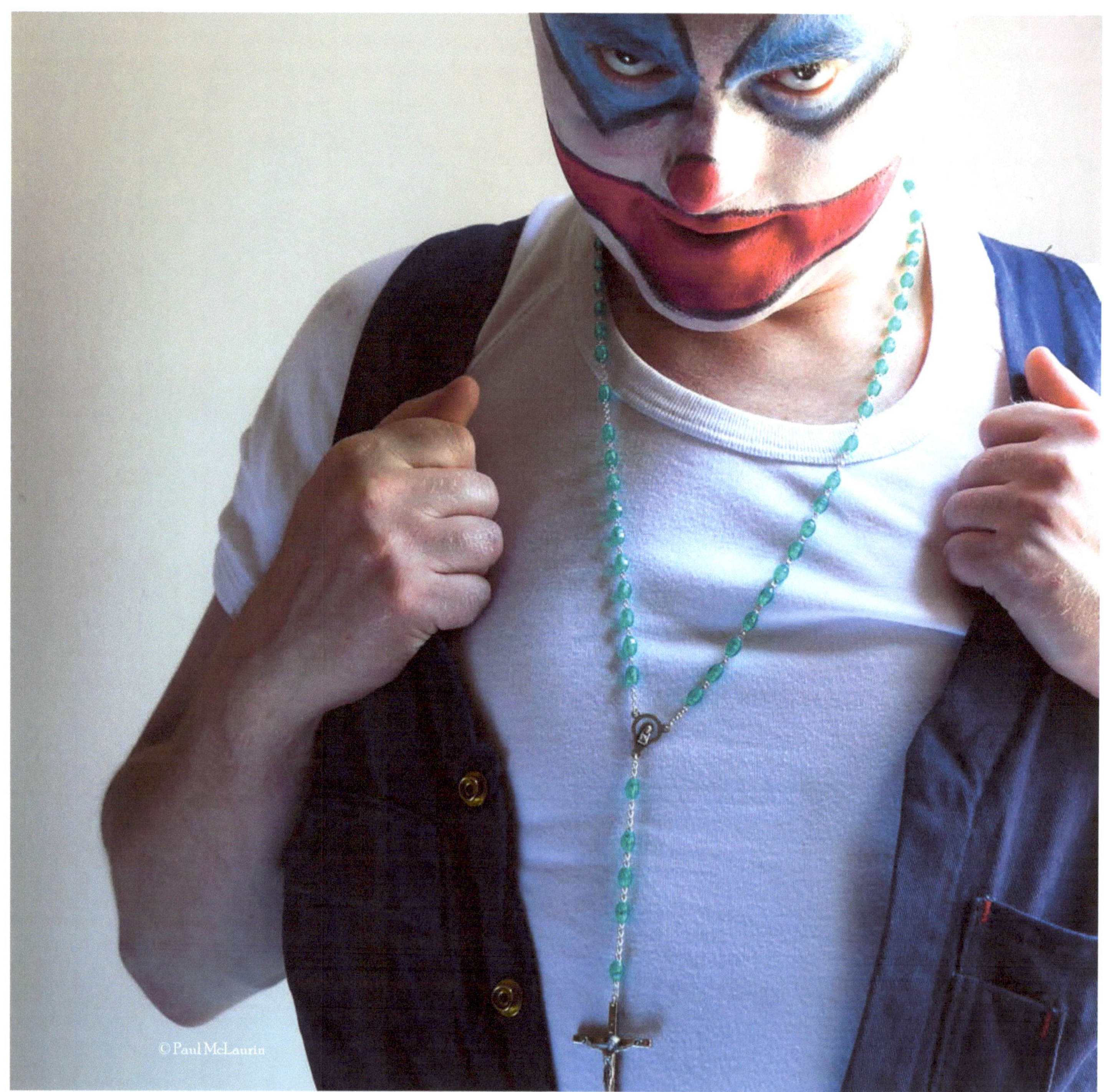
© Paul McLaurin

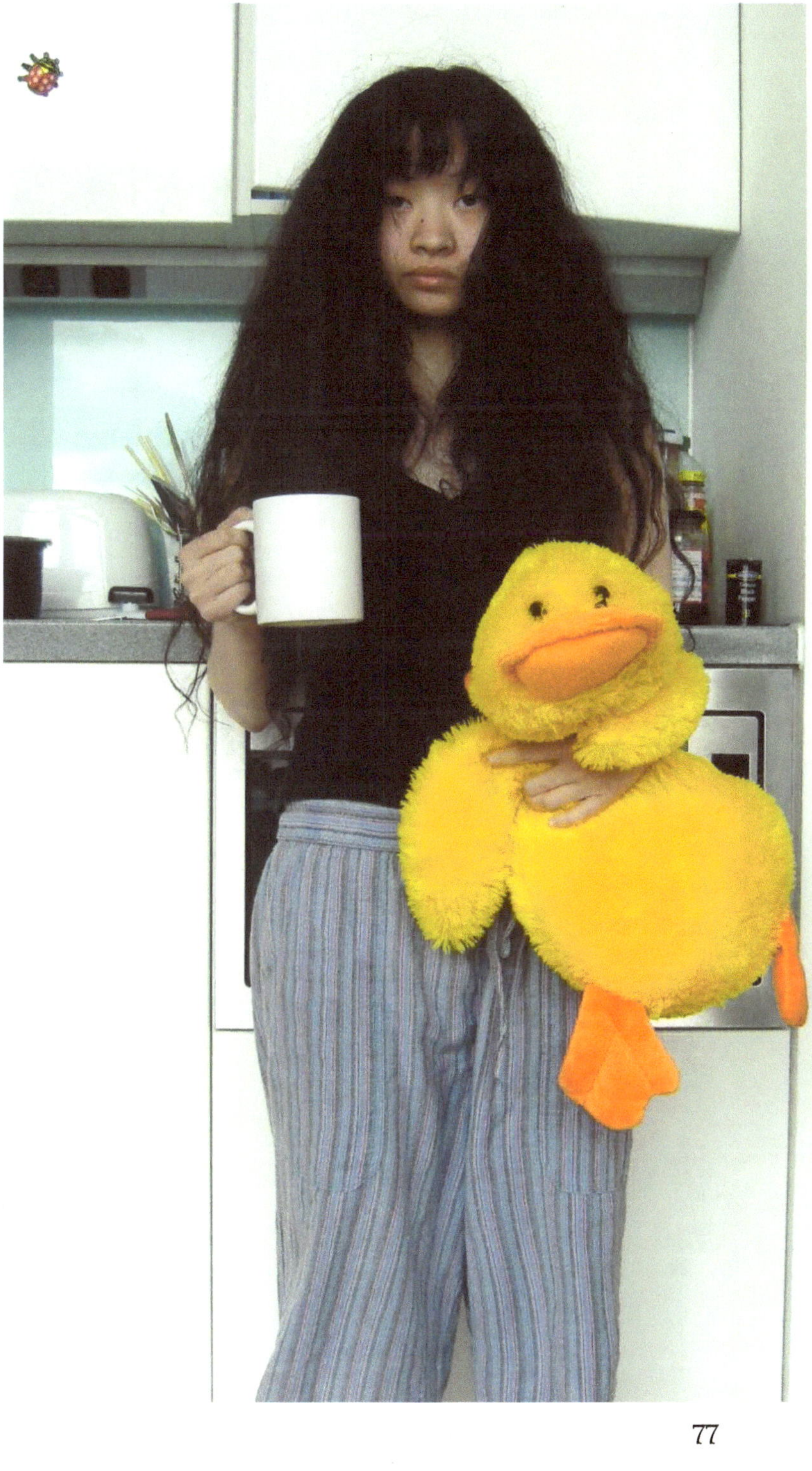

©Aven

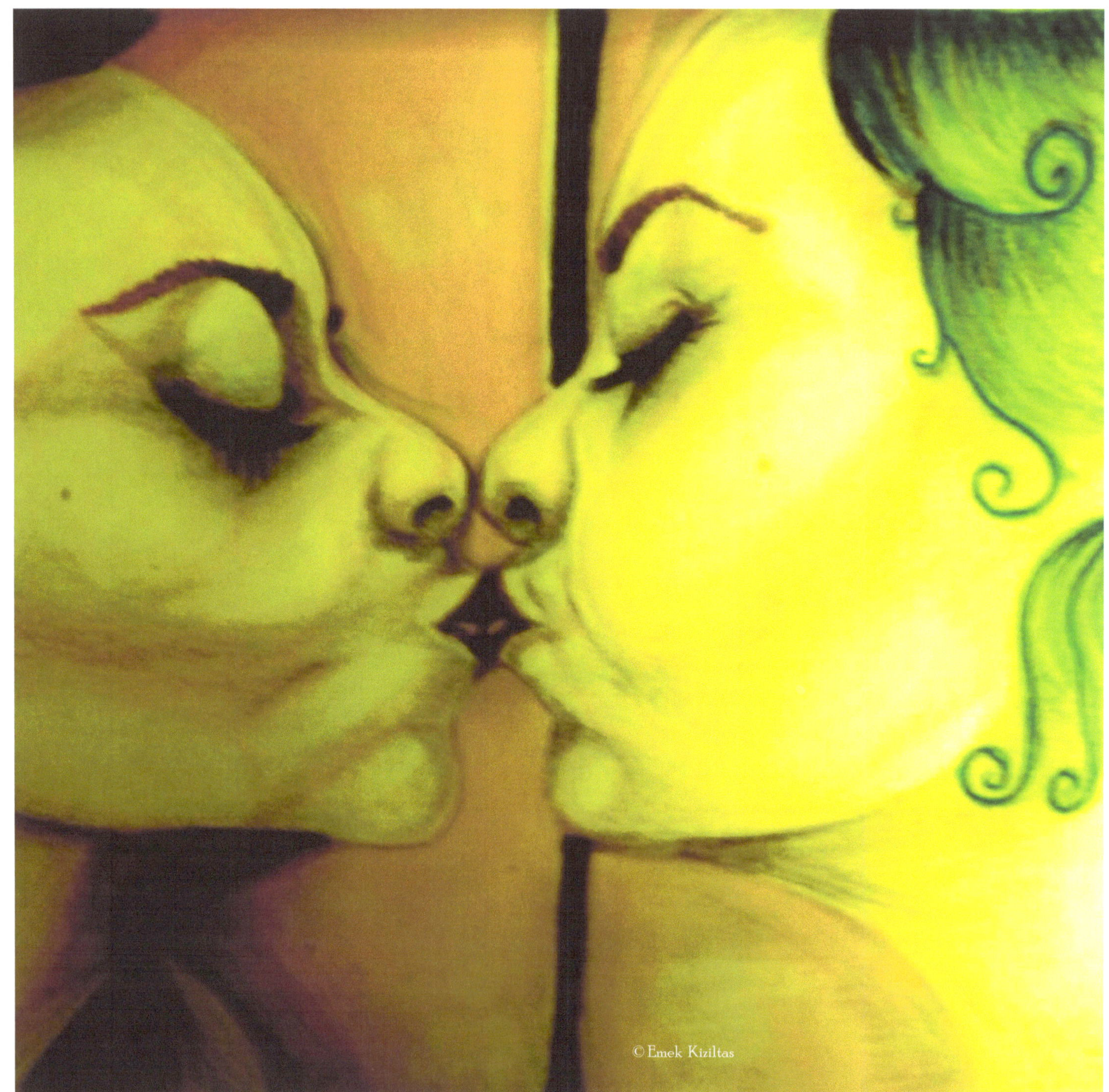

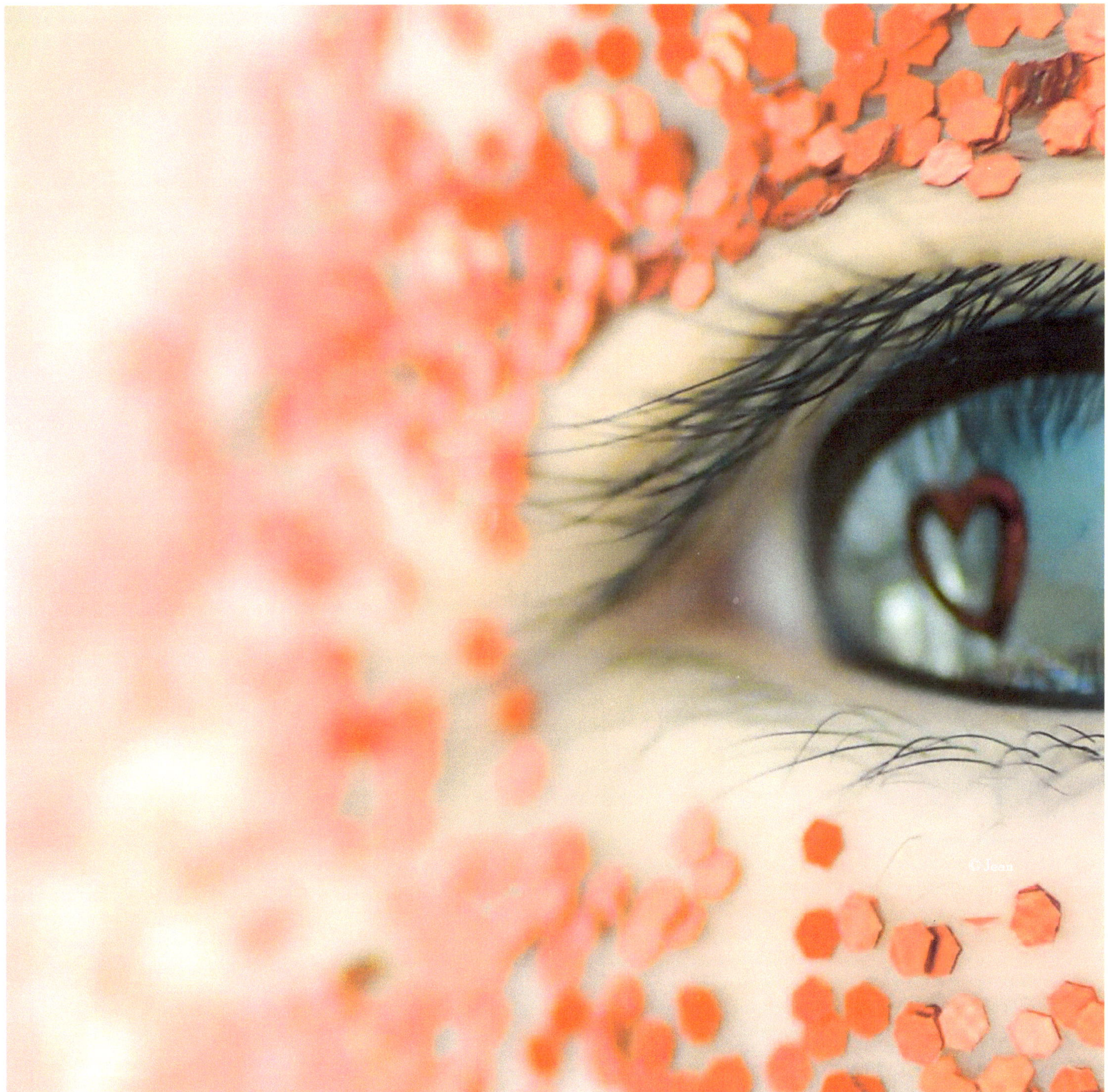
© Jean

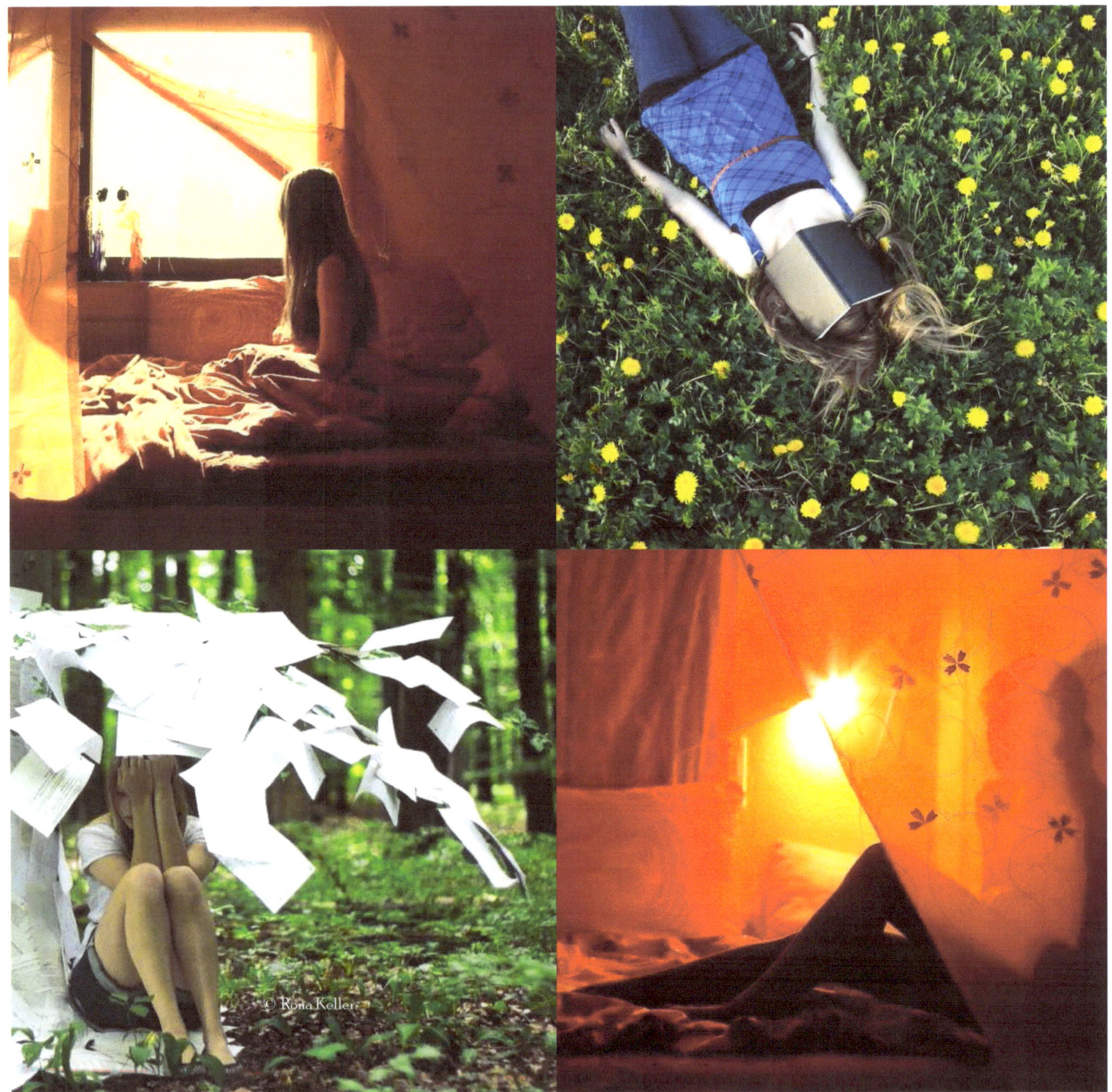
© Rona Keller

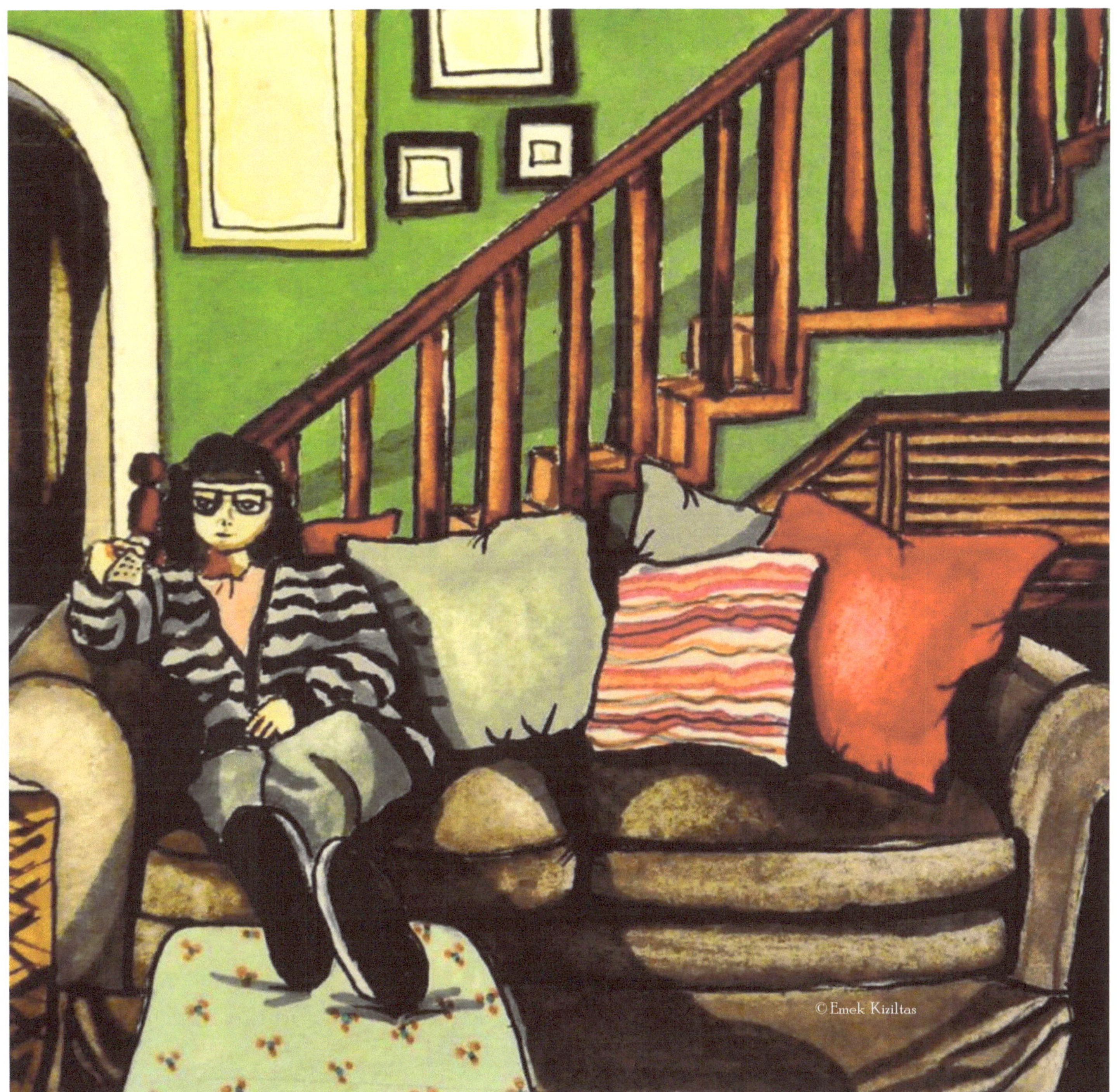
© Emek Kiziltas

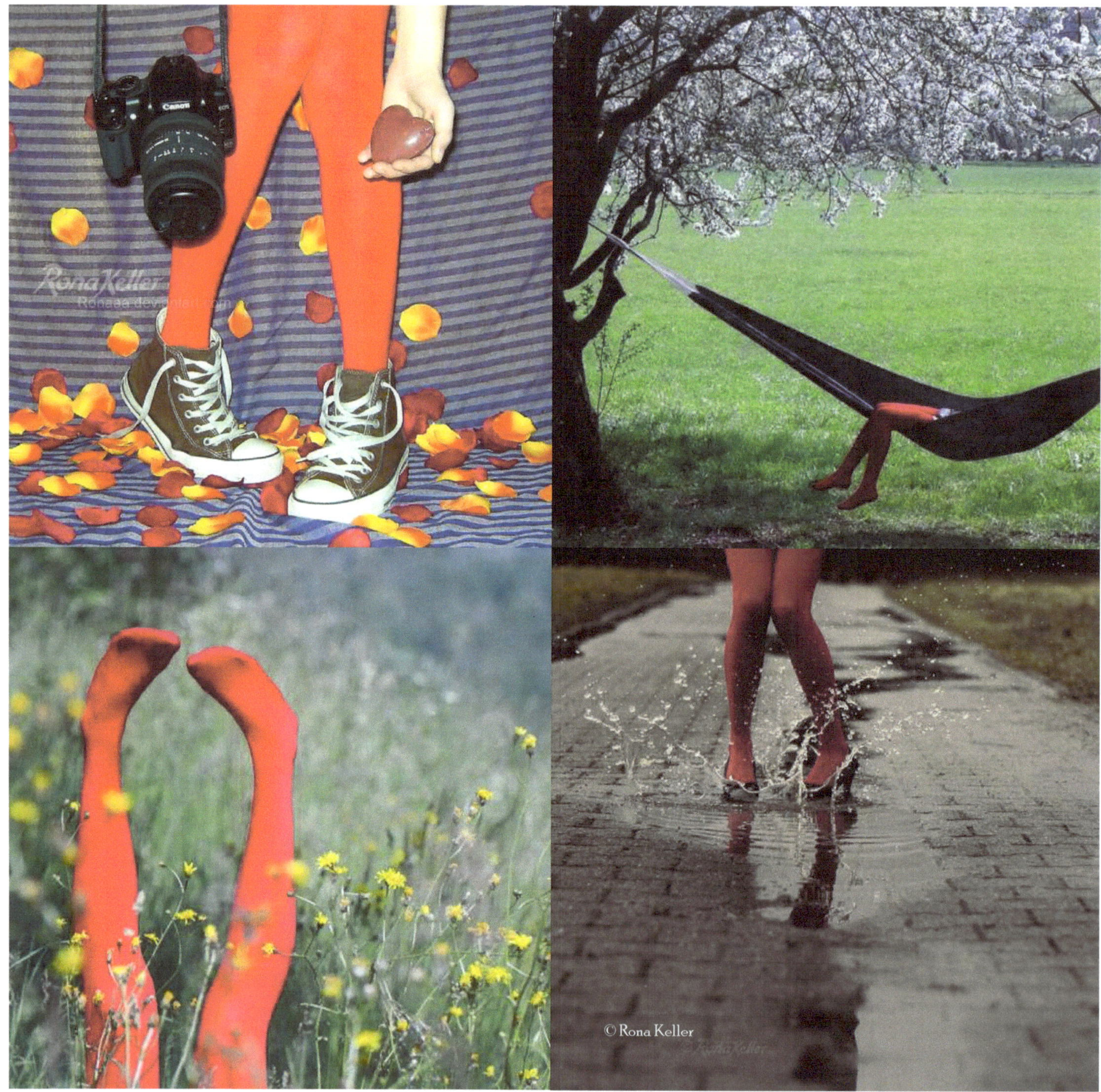
Canon
Rona Keller
© Rona Keller

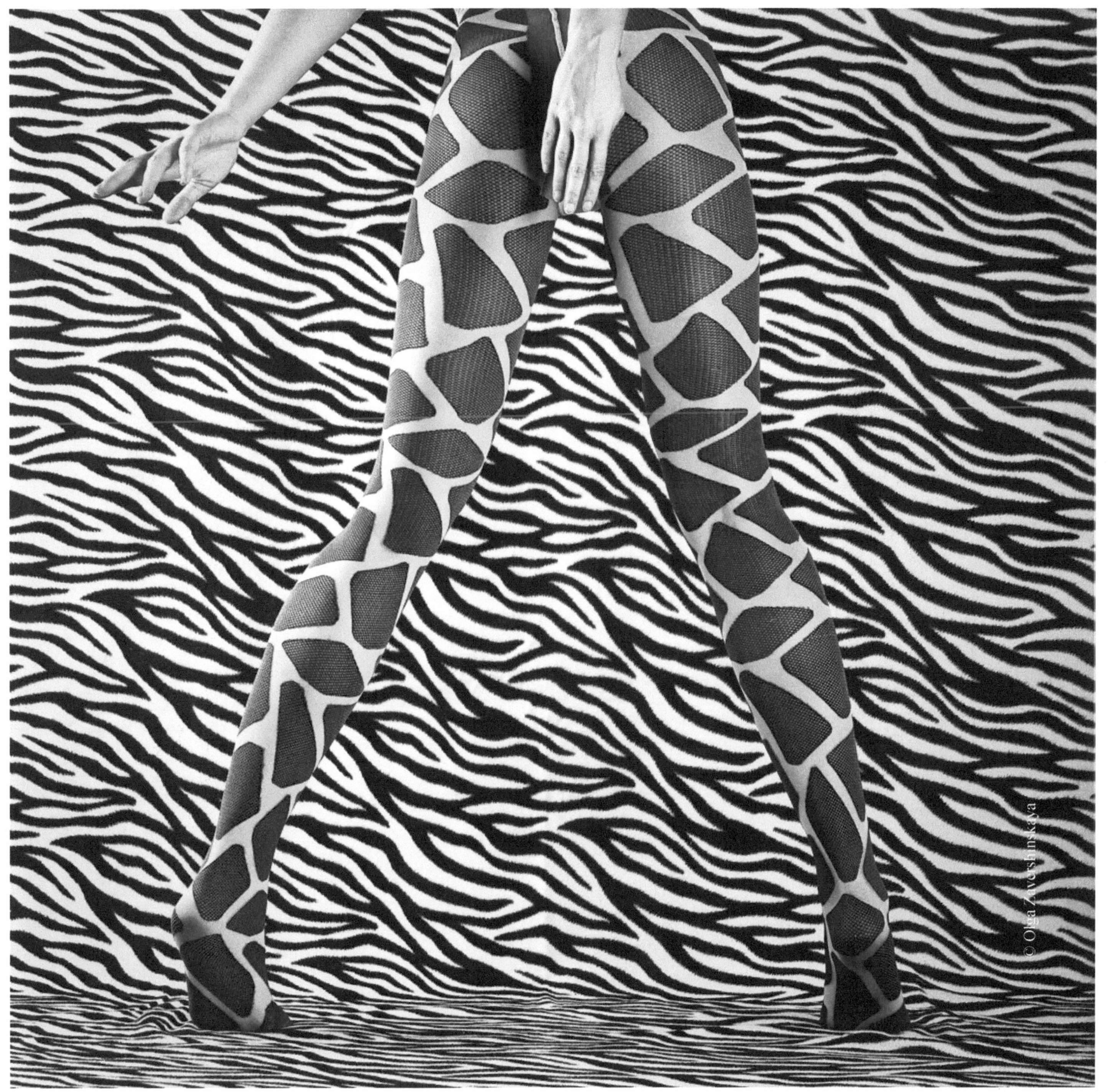
© Olga Zavershinskaya

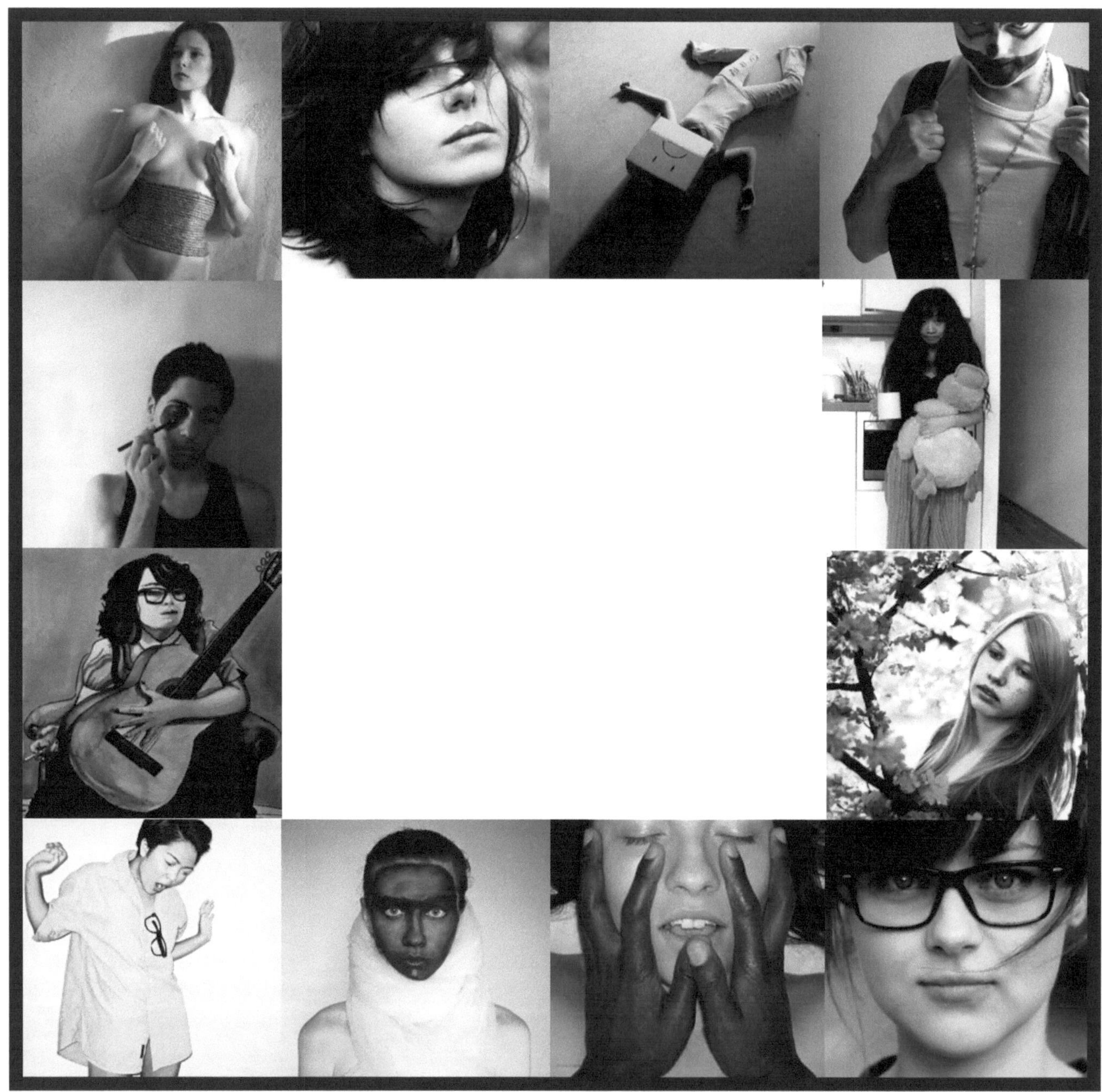

Thanks to all the Self Artists
for their contribution for this book.

www.ingramcontent.com/pod-product-compliance
Lightning Source LLC
LaVergne TN
LVHW070136110826
845147LV00002B/264

9780956489777